OPPOSING VIEWPOINTS® SERIES

Popular Culture

Other Books of Related Interest:

Opposing Viewpoints Series
Celebrity Culture

At Issue Series
Should Social Networking Web Sites Be Banned?

Current Controversies Series
Blogs

"Congress shall make
no law . . . abridging
the freedom of speech,
or of the press."

First Amendment to the U.S. Constitution

The basic foundation of our democracy is the First Amendment guarantee of freedom of expression. The Opposing Viewpoints Series is dedicated to the concept of this basic freedom and the idea that it is more important to practice it than to enshrine it.

OPPOSING
VIEWPOINTS®
SERIES

Popular Culture

David Haugen and Susan Musser, book editors

GREENHAVEN PRESS
A part of Gale, Cengage Learning

GALE
CENGAGE Learning™

Detroit • New York • San Francisco • New Haven, Conn • Waterville, Maine • London

Christine Nasso, *Publisher*
Elizabeth Des Chenes, *Managing Editor*

© 2011 Greenhaven Press, a part of Gale, Cengage Learning.

Gale and Greenhaven Press are registered trademarks used herein under license.

For more information, contact:
Greenhaven Press
27500 Drake Rd.
Farmington Hills, MI 48331-3535
Or you can visit our Internet site at gale.cengage.com

For product information and technology assistance, contact us at

Gale Customer Support, 1-800-877-4253
For permission to use material from this text or product, submit all requests online at www.cengage.com/permissions

Further permissions questions can be emailed to permissionrequest@cengage.com

Articles in Greenhaven Press anthologies are often edited for length to meet page requirements. In addition, original titles of these works are changed to clearly present the main thesis and to explicitly indicate the author's opinion. Every effort is made to ensure that Greenhaven Press accurately reflects the original intent of the authors. Every effort has been made to trace the owners of copyrighted material.

Cover Image copyright © iStockPhoto.com/Marcoscisetti.

LIBRARY OF CONGRESS CATALOGING-IN-PUBLICATION DATA

Popular culture / David Haugen and Susan Musser, book editors.
    p. cm. -- (Opposing viewpoints)
    Includes bibliographical references and index.
    ISBN 978-0-7377-4980-9 (hardcover) -- ISBN 978-0-7377-4981-6 (pbk.)
    1. Popular culture--Juvenile literature. I. Haugen, David M., 1969- II. Musser, Susan.
    HM621.P654 2010
    306--dc22

                                                            2010014754

Printed in the United States of America
1 2 3 4 5 6 7 14 13 12 11 10

Contents

Chapter 3: How Does Popular Culture Influence Society?

Chapter 4: How Is U.S. Popular Culture Received Around the World?

Why Consider Opposing Viewpoints?

> *"The only way in which a human being can make some approach to knowing the whole of a subject is by hearing what can be said about it by persons of every variety of opinion and studying all modes in which it can be looked at by every character of mind. No wise man ever acquired his wisdom in any mode but this."*
>
> John Stuart Mill

In our media-intensive culture it is not difficult to find differing opinions. Thousands of newspapers and magazines and dozens of radio and television talk shows resound with differing points of view. The difficulty lies in deciding which opinion to agree with and which "experts" seem the most credible. The more inundated we become with differing opinions and claims, the more essential it is to hone critical reading and thinking skills to evaluate these ideas. Opposing Viewpoints books address this problem directly by presenting stimulating debates that can be used to enhance and teach these skills. The varied opinions contained in each book examine many different aspects of a single issue. While examining these conveniently edited opposing views, readers can develop critical thinking skills such as the ability to compare and contrast authors' credibility, facts, argumentation styles, use of persuasive techniques, and other stylistic tools. In short, the Opposing Viewpoints Series is an ideal way to attain the higher-level thinking and reading skills so essential in a culture of diverse and contradictory opinions.

In addition to providing a tool for critical thinking, Opposing Viewpoints books challenge readers to question their own strongly held opinions and assumptions. Most people form their opinions on the basis of upbringing, peer pressure, and personal, cultural, or professional bias. By reading carefully balanced opposing views, readers must directly confront new ideas as well as the opinions of those with whom they disagree. This is not to simplistically argue that everyone who reads opposing views will—or should—change his or her opinion. Instead, the series enhances readers' understanding of their own views by encouraging confrontation with opposing ideas. Careful examination of others' views can lead to the readers' understanding of the logical inconsistencies in their own opinions, perspective on why they hold an opinion, and the consideration of the possibility that their opinion requires further evaluation.

Evaluating Other Opinions

To ensure that this type of examination occurs, Opposing Viewpoints books present all types of opinions. Prominent spokespeople on different sides of each issue as well as well-known professionals from many disciplines challenge the reader. An additional goal of the series is to provide a forum for other, less known, or even unpopular viewpoints. The opinion of an ordinary person who has had to make the decision to cut off life support from a terminally ill relative, for example, may be just as valuable and provide just as much insight as a medical ethicist's professional opinion. The editors have two additional purposes in including these less known views. One, the editors encourage readers to respect others' opinions—even when not enhanced by professional credibility. It is only by reading or listening to and objectively evaluating others' ideas that one can determine whether they are worthy of consideration. Two, the inclusion of such viewpoints encourages the important critical thinking skill of objectively evaluating an author's credentials and bias. This evaluation will illuminate an author's reasons for taking a particular stance on an issue and will aid in readers' evaluation of the author's ideas.

It is our hope that these books will give readers a deeper understanding of the issues debated and an appreciation of the complexity of even seemingly simple issues when good and honest people disagree. This awareness is particularly important in a democratic society such as ours in which people enter into public debate to determine the common good. Those with whom one disagrees should not be regarded as enemies but rather as people whose views deserve careful examination and may shed light on one's own.

Thomas Jefferson once said that "difference of opinion leads to inquiry, and inquiry to truth." Jefferson, a broadly educated man, argued that "if a nation expects to be ignorant and free . . . it expects what never was and never will be." As individuals and as a nation, it is imperative that we consider the opinions of others and examine them with skill and discernment. The Opposing Viewpoints Series is intended to help readers achieve this goal.

David L. Bender and Bruno Leone,
Founders

Introduction

> "[Since the mid-1800s], America's prime cultural tradition has been to entertain and thereby to cultivate popularity. It never had to fight to establish its legitimacy against an established high culture. . . . Ours is a popular culture of comfort and convenience. If it has any other mission than to amuse, that is to offer a populist morality—a celebration of common decencies against wicked authority."
>
> —Todd Gitlin,
> Sources, *Spring 1999*

> "Like it or not, pop culture and technology are among our most valuable exports and most identifiable brand."
>
> —Hoyt Hilsman,
> Huffington Post, *December 4, 2008*

Popular culture consists of the arts, events, trends, and people that fascinate society and tend to persist as icons in the public mind. Movies, music, celebrities, politicians, books, toys, fashions, and a host of other facets of pop culture engage the attention of society and often are discussed or referenced to show commonality of tastes. Unlike high culture, popular culture typically appeals to a broad audience that has immediate access to these artifacts, images, and stories. Thus, the media have an important role in transmitting pop culture. Whereas classic sculpture, architecture, or painting must be visited—usually in museums or other enshrined locations—to be appreciated, the latest episode of *The Simpsons* cartoon is broadcast to millions of viewers at once. The Internet is speeding the dissemination of pop culture—and high culture as well, mingling the two but ensuring overall the democratization of many art forms, narratives, and images.

To some analysts, pop culture can include any moment of collective interest in one of these elements; to others, pop culture is that that defies the fleeting fad and remains in the mass psyche for a long time. Whether pop culture requires endurance, an interest in its study has endured since the 1950s in America when the term first gained critical appreciation. Various universities now offer courses and programs in popular culture, and Washington State University, the University of Idaho, and other scholarly institutions host Web sites dedicated to analyzing and preserving pop culture. With this high regard for what social critics once regarded (and some still regard) as low culture, it is clear that pop culture has acquired prominence and even respect in recent years.

Despite the influence and reach of popular culture, many critics still deplore its leveling effect and the way it detracts from the appreciation of what they consider high art. Playwright Stephen Sewell, writing in a February 2010 edition of the Australian *Sunday Morning Herald*, argues, "While art is the province of the unexpected and the challenging, and likely to provoke incredulity and even rage, popular culture is the domain of the familiar, the mawkish, the sentimental and the trite and bears the same relationship to culture in general as a McDonald's hamburger does to food." After dismissing all low art as "rubbish," Sewell goes on to assert, "People read less, understand less and retain less than they did even 20 years ago. The mindless pap of undemanding popular culture is as responsible for this as the fast food industry is for the obesity epidemic." In Sewell's opinion—an opinion shared by many critics of pop culture—mass entertainment and faddish novelties make consumers lazy, undemanding and easily led by those who market pop culture products.

Sewell's contempt for the popular, however, is balanced by culture critics who believe that mass culture has much to recommend its consumption. Steven Johnson, the author of *Everything Bad Is Good for You: How Today's Popular Culture Is Actually Making Us Smarter*, caused a furor among pop culture naysayers when he advocated that many aspects of pop culture—including television shows, movies, and video games—actually aid the development of advanced cognitive skills. "For decades, we've worked under the assumption that mass culture follows a steadily declining path toward lowest-common-denominator standards, presumably because the 'masses' want dumb, simple pleasures and big media companies want to give the masses what they want," Johnson writes, "but in fact, the exact opposite is happening: The culture is getting more intellectually demanding, not less." In his book, Johnson explains his theory that many popular video games require players to master skills, follow open-ended storylines, and develop patience to be ultimately rewarded. He contends that good movies and television shows also demand attention to details, ask viewers to juggle several narratives and characters, and involve other high-end cognitive processes from audiences. As Johnson argues, these mental challenges are today more of a fixture of pop culture than they were fifty years ago.

American pop culture—for good or bad—is not only impacting national tastes but is spreading throughout the world thanks to the Internet and broadcast media. Since the end of World War II, the United States has focused on exporting much of its pop culture abroad with the express purpose of enticing an international audience to take an interest in and even desire American fashions, movies, television shows, music, and other arts. In this respect, American pop culture is part of the nation's "soft power" influence on the rest of the world. *Soft power* is a term used to encompass the lure of a national identity as expressed by its culture, values, and government; *hard power*, its antithesis, refers to the employment of militaries, political pressure, and aggressive policy making to manipulate foreign entities. The United States began emphasizing soft power influence during the Cold War when the American government found it easier and cheaper to make allies by sending movies, music, consumer goods, and other cultural artifacts overseas rather than sending tanks and battleships.

Political theorist Joseph S. Nye Jr. is credited with creating the term *soft power* to define these exports and influences, and he contends they are as important to American security today as they were during the Cold War. Nye asserts that in the age of Islamic terrorism, the United States should use its valuable pop culture exports to promote common understanding with those who are most vulnerable to the anti-American messages spread by terrorists. Transmitting television shows that show ethnic diversity and tolerance and using the media to highlight celebrities who work with global charities, in Nye's view, appeals to shared values among the world's citizens and does much to promote the notion that America supports a global vision of peace and social welfare. "Seduction is always more effective than coercion," Nye writes, "and many values like democracy and human rights, and individual opportunities are deeply seductive." Although American foreign policy has been widely criticized since the terrorist attacks of September 11, 2001, Nye notes that U.S. popular culture is still consumed and even admired in most parts of the world.

Despite the pervasiveness of American cultural products around the world, some critics charge that the image of America presented by these products is not as attractive as Nye would hope. In the mid-1990s, *New York Times* European culture correspondent John Rockwell wrote, "In decades past, America's chief cultural exports were debonair crooners and stalwart upholders of truth, justice and the American way. Today, a different America exports products that reflect a chilling propensity for cartoon-like, bone-crunching, eyeball-popping violence." Rockwell noted that much of what the United States was exporting in terms of movies, television shows, and music seemed to project a different kind of value system—promoting greed, violence, and sex—that did not reflect well on the nation. According to a 2007 Pew survey, this new image was not finding favor in several nations, including Russia, India, and many Islamic countries. Reporting on the survey, Diane Garrett of *Variety* stated, "In predominantly Muslim countries, it's not just that they don't approve of American culture; most plain don't like it. More than two-thirds of Bangladeshis (81%), Pakistanis (80%), Turks (68%), Palestinians (68%) and Indians (68%) said they do not like American music, movies and television." Critics worry that tarnishing the nation's image through insensitive or even offensive pop culture products may serve to heighten tensions between the United States and other nations or at best reduce global sympathy for Americans in general.

In *Opposing Viewpoints: Popular Culture*, numerous critics, analysts, and promoters of American pop culture debate these national and global issues. In chapters titled Does Popular Culture Have Value?, How Has the Internet Impacted Popular Culture?, How Does Popular Culture Influence Society?, and How Is U.S. Popular Culture Received Around the World?, these experts address various aspects of popular culture and their influence on American society and the world at large. Some bemoan the fall of high culture, while others believe the spread of pop culture on a national or global scale brings people together by giving them shared points of reference. Despite the debate over the value of pop culture, it is evident that America's pop culture has a great deal of influence at home and abroad, impacting not only discussions about the supposed distinctions between low and high art but also affecting the ways in which culture is transmitted and consumed across the planet.

CHAPTER 1

Does Popular Culture Have Value?

Chapter Preface

In a 2005 article for the *Wilson Quarterly*, James Morris proclaims his personal predilection for television entertainment over movie theater offerings. While admitting that television programming "has always been mostly awful," Morris asserts that "there's a case to be made that, on many evenings, an intelligent adult is better off spending an hour or two in front of a TV set than in a movie theater." He maintains that Hollywood fare and independent films alike lack the qualities to engage adult viewers. On the other hand, he attests that many popular television programs "can now teach Hollywood something about smarts."

Morris points to comedy shows such as the now-defunct *Everybody Loves Raymond* and *Arrested Development* as primetime examples of well-written situation comedies that deconstruct family relationships, and he acknowledges the animated *Simpsons* and *King of the Hill* as irreverent reminders of political and social flaws in the fabric of America. Morris also offers up the drama *24* as a successful combination of action and thought-provoking, what-if theorizing that "knows how to tell a story—indeed, to tell many stories at once." He then goes on to praise other programs for their witty dialogue and universal themes. "What I admire most about these shows, and most deplore about contemporary movies, is the quality of the scripts," Morris states, explaining that television programs are forced to foreground human interaction because they cannot compete with the special effects barrages that clutter up the big screen.

Morris also insists that television characters are better drawn than their film counterparts—primarily because the serialized nature of broadcasts allows for character development over time. "Their lives and circumstances achieve a cumulative familiarity, in which viewers are invested," he writes, "and the familiar comes to exert a comfortable pull, which yields to a what-happens-next curiosity." The cumulative familiarity is part of what gives television shows value for Morris. Viewers return again and again to favorite shows because they are ensured the engaging characters, well-written scripts, and interesting storylines will return again and again. While Morris does not claim there are no good movies, he simply believes that many modern movies do not provide that same kind of value offered on television. Instead, he laments that too many movies are either mindless drivel targeted at young people or self-important social criticism that alienates audiences hoping to be entertained.

In the following chapter, the authors examine other facets of popular culture to assess the worth of the mediums and the messages. Like the two sides of Morris's comparative analysis, some see value in what is often disparaged as the trendy and the trivial, while others seek to dismiss pop culture offerings as distracting and empty pursuits for audiences that fail to demand more of art and culture.

| *"Personal Journalism is just as ethical as old-school public journalism."*

Blogging Is Journalism

Howard Owens

Howard Owens has been a journalist for more than two decades. Since September 2006, Owens has been director of digital publishing for GateHouse Media, Inc., and he runs the online version of the Batavian, *a New York newspaper. In the following viewpoint taken from his personal blog, Owens argues that the personal computer, the Internet, and mobile communication devices have given writers the ability to report stories that interest them and reach millions of equally interested readers. This is a new breed of journalism that retains the facts and truth telling of traditional journalism, he contends, but lays bare the bias of the author. These "personal journalists," as Owens calls committed Web log (blog) writers, participate in large discussions, culling news and information from many sources and distilling it for their audience. Owens believes all journalism will soon adopt this model because readers seem to respond well to it.*

Howard Owens, "Personal Journalism," howardowens.com, January 23, 2007. Reproduced by permission.

As you read, consider the following questions:

1. How are personal computers, mobile phones, iPods, and digital video recorders inherently different forms of media devices compared with televisions and radios, according to Owens?

2. What aspect of personal journalism does the author think all journalism should "endorse"?

3. How long (since the January 2007 publication of this viewpoint) does Owens think it will take for all journalism to switch to the personal model?

Over the past few days [in January 2007], I keep flashing back on a blog post by Pete Townshend [guitarist for the rock band The Who] titled "Open letter to David Lister." I've referenced it in conversations with colleagues, and I was thinking of it when I wrote this post on video and personal communication.

Townshend:

> I think rock music is about to throw off some of its testosterone-driven defiance. I may be wrong, but wherever I look today I see younger musicians demanding a new level of intimacy from their audience. 'Unplugged' rock is not exactly what is happening. It is more a return to the traditions of Bert Jansch, Pete Seeger, Woody Guthrie, Ewan McColl, Dave Van Ronk, Big Bill Broonzy, Joan Baez and even early Bob Dylan. This is not entirely about Protest, rather about music performed gently that expresses a single idea along the single pathway of the conscience of an individual musician daring to speak up about something they might uniquely believe. Even anger is delivered gently.

Every where I turn today, I see media that is more intimate and more immediate taking root and growing strong. It's not just music, though I see it in *Paste Magazine* and hear it on XM Cafe. I read it in blogs, watch it in the best YouTube

The Rise of Placeblogging

Community blogs are having a sizable impact on traditional journalism. Many serve a watchdog function, just as investigative reporters from the "legacy" media used to do (and sometimes still do, newsroom budgets and corporate ties permitting). . . . Some civic-minded bloggers take a critical tone with local government; others are less combative. But no matter what the prevailing tone, these blogs give readers a rich sense of place.

In fact, "placebloggers" is the collective name for the citizens who generate locally driven blogs and news sites. A Zogby survey released in February 2008 found that 70 percent of Americans say journalism is important to maintaining community quality of life, but that nearly as high a number—67 percent—say the traditional media are out of touch with what citizens want out of their news. Bill Densmore of the Media Giraffe Project at the University of Massachusetts–Amherst says the rise in community blogs has happened as local newspapers cut staff, adding, "People hunger for community, but the economic reality of the mainstream media is that they can't supply that need anymore, or choose not to."

Julie Fanselow, National Civic Review, *Winter 2008.*

videos, vlogs and independent films. I view it in photo sharing sites. It's what drives social networking. People are reaching out to touch other people, not be impressed by concepts or ideologies, wowed by trends or gather just one more factoid. They want the human spirit and the human soul.

Personal Technology, Personal Meaning

I tried to express this before: The personal computer, a mobile phone, an iPod, a DVR, etc. are all intimately personal devices. The radios and televisions we grew up with were shared experiences. They captured a transitory signal, and if we happened to tune in at the right moment, we knew what was seen and heard was being simultaneously seen and heard by others. When the signal was gone, the moment was gone. We could only recapture it in a personal way when we gathered around the water cooler.

A cassette or VHS tape made media somewhat more personal and shareable, but we still lacked a certain level of control.

Digital technology changes everything. Now, what we download, we own. When it arrives on our computer screen, it is ours to keep, if we want.

Once we own something, it changes our relationship with it. We want it to mean something to us. We want to interact with it, mix it or answer it.

For that segment of the web audience who has tuned into the power of blogs, I think this is what has energized their passion for blogging. The best bloggers write in individual voices. We know they're real people. We feel like we can engage in a conversation and get an answer.

I'm coming to the conclusion that the new journalism is Personal Journalism.

Personal Journalism Is Still Good Reporting

Personal Journalism is just as ethical as old-school public journalism. It still values facts, fairness, truth telling and good reporting. It's just that personal journalism is written differently. It is written from one person, a person we can identify and identify with, for one person. The byline is more than a name under a headline in Personal Journalism. It is the persona and the personality. Personal journalists do more than report the story. They let us see at least a little about who they are, what they believe, what drives them and what they find important. If a personal journalist has a bias, we know it. That is part of the truth-telling tradition all journalists should endorse, but only personal journalists make it a practice.

Personal Journalism is shareable because people like to share what has touched them in a direct, intimate way, be it a song, a video or a good story.

Personal Journalists let other people help with the fact gathering or putting the facts in context, because Personal Journalism is part of a conversation, not a proprietary, walled garden.

Personal journalists can be writers, recorders or picture takers, but for the sake of clarity, I've written the definition from a writer's point of view.

Personal Journalism Will Survive

In the future, all journalists will be personal journalists. Within five to ten years, if you're not a personal journalist, you will be out of work, and if your news organization hasn't embraced personal journalism, it will be out of business. Well, that may be going a bit too far, because I'm not sure personal journalism is required of those who report for print or broadcast, but it is required of online journalists. So long as print survives, even in newsletters for the elderly and the elite, public journalism will survive. In the online world, personal journalism will be the only journalism people consistently seek.

In the past, I've struggled for the right words to describe where I see journalism going. I think with the term Personal Journalism and my proposed definition, I might be on to something.

UPDATE: Having slept on it a night, I think—maybe this isn't something we adopt or impose, maybe it is just how we evolve. Maybe it's inevitable. But then I think, but if this is where the audience is going, and it's what our disruptors do (such as blogs), then if we don't consciously make the switch, can we survive?

"One gets the uneasy sense that the blog-osphere is a potpourri of opinion and little more."

Blogging Is Not Journalism

Michael Skube

In the following viewpoint, Michael Skube draws a distinction between journalists and bloggers. While Skube credits bloggers for expanding the national debate on many important issues, he contends that blogging typically lacks the fact checking, information gathering, and dedication to quality coverage that journalism strives to embody. Skube believes that bloggers should not be termed journalists because their purpose often is to provide "armchair commentary" instead of in-depth reporting. Michael Skube began writing editorials for the North Carolina Raleigh News & Observer *in 1982 before joining the* Atlanta Journal-Constitution *in the mid-1990s. He won a Pulitzer Prize in Criticism for book reviews he penned for the* News & Observer.

As you read, consider the following questions:

1. What does the acronym MSM stand for, as Skube reports, and how do different groups interpret its meaning?

2. What 2006 legal victory does the author say afforded bloggers some recognition as journalists?

3. Why does Skube argue that only a journalist, not a blogger, could have exposed the problems at the Walter Reed Army Medical Center in 2007?

The late Christopher Lasch once wrote that public affairs generally and journalism in particular suffered not from too little information but from entirely too much. What was needed, he argued, was robust debate. Lasch, a historian by training but a cultural critic by inclination, was writing in 1990, when the Internet was not yet a part of everyday life and bloggers did not exist.

Bloggers now are everywhere among us, and no one asks if we don't need more full-throated advocacy on the Internet. The blogosphere is the loudest corner of the Internet, noisy with disputation, manifesto-like postings and an unbecoming hatred of enemies real and imagined.

Bloggers Claiming the Title of Journalists

And to think most bloggers are doing all this on the side. "No man but a blockhead," the stubbornly sensible Samuel Johnson said, "ever wrote but for money." Yet here are people, whole brigades of them, happy to write for free. And not just write. Many of the most active bloggers—Andrew Sullivan, Matthew Yglesias, Joshua Micah Marshall and the contributors to the Huffington Post—are insistent partisans in political debate. Some reject the label "journalist," associating it with what they contemptuously call MSM (mainstream media); just as many, if not more, consider themselves a new kind of "citizen journalist" dedicated to broader democratization.

Markos Moulitsas Zuniga, whose popular blog Daily Kos has been a force among antiwar activists, cautioned bloggers last week [in August 2007] "to avoid the right-wing acronym MSM." It implied, after all, that bloggers were on the fringe.

To the contrary, he wrote, "we are representatives of the main-stream, and the country is embracing what we're selling."

Moulitsas foresees bloggers becoming the watchdogs that watch the watchdog: "We need to keep the media honest, but as an institution, it's important that they exist and do their job well." The tone is telling: breezy, confident, self-congratulatory. Subtly, it implies bloggers have all the liberties of a traditional journalist but few of the obligations.

There is at least some reason for activists like Moulitsas to see themselves as the new wave. Last year, [in 2006,] the California 6th District Court of Appeal gave bloggers the legal victory they wanted when it ruled that they were protected under the state's reporter shield law. Other, more symbolic victories have come their way too. In 2004, bloggers were awarded press credentials to the Democratic National Convention. And earlier this month [August 2007] in Chicago, at a convention sponsored by Daily Kos, a procession of Democratic presidential hopefuls offered full salutes, knowing that bloggers are busy little bees in organizing political support and fundraising.

And yet none of this makes them journalists, even in the sense Lasch seemed to be advocating.

Valuing Opinion over Story

"What democracy requires," Lasch wrote in "The Lost Art of Argument," "is vigorous public debate, not information. Of course, it needs information too, but the kind of information it needs can only be generated by debate. We do not know what we need until we ask the right questions, and we can identify the right questions only by subjecting our own ideas about the world to the test of public controversy."

There was something appealing about this argument—one that no blogger would reject—when Lasch advanced it almost two decades ago. But now we have the opportunity to witness it in practice, thanks to the blogosphere, and the results are

The Grandiose Dreams of Blog Critics

Big plans and big claims are to be expected from folks—pajama-clad or not—who are dabbling with new technology and new modalities of public expression. As a retired mainstream media ("MSM") journalist—and thus a double-dinosaur—I don't begrudge these knights of the blog-table their grandiose dreams. But I worked on a school paper when I was a kid and I owned a CB radio when I lived in Texas. And what I saw in the blogosphere on Nov. 2 [2004, when exit polls for the presidential election were released and debated] was more reminiscent of that school paper or a "Breaker, breaker 19" gabfest on CB than anything approaching journalism.

Eric Engberg, CBS News,
November 8, 2004. www.cbsnews.com.

less than satisfying. One gets the uneasy sense that the blogosphere is a potpourri of opinion and little more. The opinions are occasionally informed, often tiresomely cranky and never in doubt. Skepticism, restraint, a willingness to suspend judgment and to put oneself in the background—these would not seem to be a blogger's trademarks.

But they are, more often than not, trademarks of the kind of journalism that makes a difference. And if there is anything bloggers want more than an audience, it's knowing they are making a difference in politics. They are, to give them their due, changing what is euphemistically called the national "conversation." But what is the nature of that change? Does it deepen our understanding? Does it broaden our perspective?

It's hard to answer yes to such questions, if only because they presuppose a curiosity and inquiry for which raw opinion is ill-suited. Sometimes argument—a word that elevates blogosphere comment to a level it seldom attains on its own—gains from old-fashioned gumshoe reporting. Compelling examples abound. On the same day I read of the Daily Kos convention in Chicago, I finished "The Race Beat: The Press, the Civil Rights Struggle and the Awakening of a Nation," winner this year of the Pulitzer Prize for history. No one looms larger in the book by Gene Roberts Jr. and Hank Klibanoff than Claude Sitton, whose reporting in the *New York Times* in the 1960s would become legendary.

Full disclosure: I once worked for Sitton at the *News & Observer* in Raleigh, N.C., after he had left the *Times*, and I knew that he and others, including Karl Fleming, had put themselves in harm's way simply to report a story. I naively asked Sitton once if he had encountered veiled threats. "Veiled?" he asked. "They were more than veiled."

He recounted the time in Philadelphia, Miss., when "a few rednecks—drunk, shotguns in the back of their truck—showed up at the Holiday Inn where Fleming and I were staying." The locals invited the big-city reporters—Sitton from the *Times*, Fleming from *Newsweek*—to come out and see the farm. "I told 'em, 'Look, you shoot us and there'll be a dozen more just like us in the morning. You going to shoot them too?'"

When I knew him, Sitton seldom mentioned those dangers of 20 years earlier. What mattered was the story, and the people swept up in it. But it was his vivid, detailed reporting that, as Roberts and Klibanoff write, caught the attention of the [John F.] Kennedy White House and brought the federal government to intervene in a still-segregated South.

The Need for a Commitment to Reporting

In our time, the *Washington Post*'s reporting, in late 2005, of the CIA's [Central Intelligence Agency] secret overseas prisons and its painstaking reports this year on problems [concerning the deterioration of the facility and the neglect of patients] at

Walter Reed Army Medical Center—both of which won Pulitzer Prizes—were not exercises in armchair commentary. The disgrace at Walter Reed, true enough, was first mentioned in a blog, but the full scope of that story could not have been undertaken by a blogger or, for that matter, an Op-Ed columnist, whose interest is in expressing an opinion quickly and pungently. Such a story demanded time, thorough fact-checking and verification and, most of all, perseverance. It's not something one does as a hobby.

The more important the story, the more incidental our opinions become. Something larger is needed: the patient sifting of fact, the acknowledgment that assertion is not evidence and, as the best writers understand, the depiction of real life. Reasoned argument, as well as top-of-the-head comment on the blogosphere, will follow soon enough, and it should. But what lodges in the memory, and sometimes knifes us in the heart, is the fidelity with which a writer observes and tells. The word has lost its luster, but we once called that reporting.

| *"Reality TV presents some of the most vital political debate in America, particularly about class and race."* |

Reality Television Has Value

Michael Hirschorn

Michael Hirschorn is executive vice president of original programming and production for VH1 and has produced many of that cable channel's reality programs. In the following viewpoint, Hirschorn defends reality television as a creative force that offers an alternative to stale-plotted dramas and comedies. He contends that in addition to providing lively entertainment, reality television presents real characters who engage with social issues, such as race, gender, and politics. Hirschorn believes the boom in reality programming fits well alongside the socially engaging film documentaries of the past decade, which have undertaken novel approaches to grapple with pressing issues and emotional truths.

As you read, consider the following questions:

1. What critique does Hirschorn offer of procedural dramas such as *Law & Order, CSI*, and *Criminal Minds*?

2. What praise does the author give to the reality show *The Real Housewives of Orange County*?

3. How does Hirschorn think all creative endeavors—written, scripted, or produced—should be measured?

This past January [2007], I had the pleasure of serving as official spear-catcher for a *CBS Evening News* report on the increasing levels of humiliation on *American Idol* [AI] and other reality-TV shows, including some on my channel, VH1. The segment featured snippets of our shows *I Love New York* (a dating competition with an urban vibe) and *Celebrity Fit Club* (which tracks the efforts of overweight singers and actors to get back in shape, and, by extension, reignite their careers). "VH1, among other things, showcases faded celebrities who are fat," said the CBS correspondent Richard Schlesinger.

In between shots of me fake working at my computer and fake chatting with the amiable Schlesinger while fake strolling down our corporate-looking hallway, I took my best shot at defending the alleged horrors of *AI* and *Celebrity Fit Club*. But it was clear that CBS News was set on bemoaning what it saw as yet another outrage against the culture. The central complaint, per [CBS news anchor] Katie Couric's intro to the report, was that more people had watched *American Idol* the previous week than watched the State of the Union address on all the broadcast networks combined. When the segment ended, Couric signed off with an extravagant eye roll. "We're doing our part here at CBS News," she seemed to be saying, "but the barbarians are massing at the gates, people." A line had been drawn in the sand, as if the news were now akin to an evening at the Met [the Metropolitan Opera in New York City].

A Cost-Effective, Lively Genre

Is there an easier position to take in polite society than to patronize reality TV? Even television programmers see the genre as a kind of visual Hamburger Helper: cheap filler that saves them money they can use elsewhere for more-worthy programming. Reality shows cost anywhere from a quarter to half as much to produce as scripted shows. The money saved on *Extreme Makeover: Home Edition*, the logic goes, allows ABC to pay for additional gruesome medical emergencies and exploding ferries on *Grey's Anatomy*. NBC's crappy *Fear Factor* pays for the classy *Heroes*.

As befits a form driven largely by speed and cost considerations, reality TV is not often formally daring. Fifteen years after MTV's *The Real World* set the template for contemporary reality TV by placing seven strangers in a downtown Manhattan loft, reality television has developed its own visual shorthand: short doses of documentary footage interspersed with testimonials (often called OTFs, for "on-the-fly" interviews) in which the participants describe, ex post facto, what they were thinking during the action you are watching.

The current boom may be a product of the changing economics of the television business, but reality TV is also the liveliest genre on the set right now. It has engaged hot-button cultural issues—class, sex, race—that respectable television, including the august *CBS Evening News*, rarely touches. And it has addressed a visceral need for a different kind of television at a time when the Web has made more traditionally produced video seem as stagey as [seventeenth-century French playwright] Molière.

Reality TV may be an awkward mixture of documentary (with its connotations of thousands of hours of footage patiently gathered, redacted by monk-like figures into the purest expression of truth possible in 90 to 120 minutes) and scripted (with its auteurs and Emmys and noble overtones of craft), but this kludge also happens to have allowed reality shows to skim the best elements of scripted TV and documentaries while eschewing the problems of each. Reality shows steal the story structure and pacing of scripted television, but leave behind the canned plots and characters. They have the visceral impact of documentary reportage without the self-importance and general lugubriousness. Where documentaries must construct their narratives from found matter, reality TV can place real people in artificial surroundings designed for maximum emotional impact.

A Vibrant Alternative to Tired Dramas

Scripted television is supposedly showing new ambition these days, particularly in the hour-long drama form. *Studio 60 on the Sunset Strip* was going to bring the chatty intelligence of *The West Wing* back to prime time. *Lost* was going to challenge network audiences like never before, with complex plots, dozens of recurring characters, and movie-level production values. Shows are bigger now: On *24* this season, a nuclear bomb exploded. But network prime-time television remains dominated by variants on the police procedural (*Law & Order*, *CSI*, *Criminal Minds*), in which a stock group of characters (ethnically, sexually, and generationally diverse) grapples with endless versions of the same dilemma. The episodes have all the ritual predictability of Japanese Noh theater: Crimes are solved, lessons are learned, order is restored.

Reality shows have leaped into this imaginative void. Discovery's *Deadliest Catch*, which began its third season in April [2007], is an oddly transfixing series about . . . crab fishermen in the Bering Sea. As a straightforward documentary, *Catch* would have been worthy fodder, but the producers have made it riveting by formatting the whole season as a sporting event, with crab tallies for each of the half dozen or so boats and a race-against-the-clock urgency that, for all its contrivance, gives structure and meaning to the fishermen's efforts.

Narrative vibrancy is not the only thing that electrifies these shows. Reality TV presents some of the most vital political debate in America, particularly about class and race. Fox's *Nanny 911* and ABC's *Supernanny* each offer object lessons on the hazards of parenting in an age of instant gratification and endless digital diversion. ABC's *Extreme Makeover: Home Edi-*

Most Popular Reality Television Shows by Viewer Ratings

Show	Network
1. MythBusters	Discovery
2. The Amazing Race	CBS
3. Viva la Bam	MTV3
4. How It's Made	The Science Channel
5. Most Extreme Elimination Challenge	Spike TV
6. I Love The 80's	VH1
7. Ghost Hunters	SyFy
8. Little People, Big World	TLC
9. Criss Angel Mindfreak	A&E
10. Rob & Big	MTV
11. Survivorman	Discovery
12. Dirty Jobs	Discovery
13. Kathy Griffin: My Life on the D-List	Bravo
14. Extreme Makeover: Home Edition	ABC
15. Man vs. Wild	Discovery
16. It Takes a Thief (2005)	Discovery
17. The Mole	ABC
18. Miami Ink	TLC
19. Endurance	Discovery Kids
20. Kitchen Nightmares	FOX

TAKEN FROM: TV.com, "Most Popular Reality Shows of All Time by Rating," January 24, 2010. www.tv.com.

tion features intensely emotional tales of people who have fallen through the cracks of [George W.] Bush-era America—often blue-collar families ravaged by disease, health-care costs, insurance loopholes, layoffs, and so forth. My channel's *The (White) Rapper Show* turned into a running debate among the aspiring white MCs over cultural authenticity—whether it is more properly bestowed by class or race.

Getting at Real Issues

Class realities are plumbed to remarkable effect on *The Real Housewives of Orange County*, a "docu soap" that completed its second season on Bravo this spring. The show is inspired by a trio of suburban dramas: *The O.C.*, *Desperate Housewives*, and the 1999 movie *American Beauty*. Lacking the visual panache, or the budgets, of its scripted forebears, *Real Housewives* nonetheless goes deeper, charting the spiritual decay of life in gated communities, where financial anxieties, fraying families, and fear of aging leave inhabitants grasping for meaning and happiness as they steer their Escalades across Southern California's perfectly buffed, featureless landscape. *Crash*, the 2006 Oscar winner, trafficked in similar white California dread, but with all the nuance of a two-by-four to the face.

In *Real Housewives*, businessman Lou Knickerbocker stages a photo shoot to promote his new "highly oxygenated" water, variously called "Aqua Air" and "O.C. Energy Drink" ("We have patented technology that produces water from air"). The models are attractive-ish teen and 20-something girls: Lou's daughter Lindsey, by ex-wife Tammy; a few other daughters of O.C. housewives; and a newcomer whom Lou apparently found waitressing at a local restaurant.

Lou and Tammy made piles of money—it's not clear how—but their finances seem to have fractured along with their marriage. The photo shoot, therefore, is throwing off more than the normal amount of flop sweat. Lou apparently has personally selected the girls, which means he has declined to showcase his other daughter, Megan, because of her tattoos and lack of physical fitness. Lou believes the "Aqua Air Angels" should embody the Aqua Air ideal, which is why they can't drink or smoke and must have grade-point averages higher than 3.5. "This is a photo shoot," he barks after a fight breaks out between one of the girls and the waitress, "not a gang bang, for chrissakes."

The detail is what puts the scene over: Lou's lip-smacking focus on the girls, the girls' bland acquiescence. "That's it, baby, smile," Lou urges his daughter. "Show those teeth," says Tammy. A similar scenario on *Desperate Housewives* could never have been quite this preposterous, quite this blandly amoral. The characters would have been scripted with softening, redeeming qualities, or been rendered comically evil. Lou would've gotten his comeuppance, like Wallace Shawn's money-siphoning literary agent in that series. Here, the apparent willingness of the young women and at least some of the parents to indulge Lou's bottom-of-the-barrel scheming outlines, in a few short brushstrokes, a community's shared value system.

Rendering Emotional Truths

Value systems are smashed into each other, like atoms in an accelerator, on ABC's *Wife Swap*, where the producers find the most extreme pairings possible: lesbian mommies with bigots, godless cosmopolites with Bible thumpers. On one February [2007] show, a Pentacostal family, the Hoovers, was paired with the family of a former pastor, Tony Meeks, who has turned from God to follow his rock-and-roll dreams (mom Tish rocks out as well). "I feel by being there," Kristin Hoover said, "I was able to remind Tony that God still loves him and is not finished with him." The episode took seriously the Hoovers' commitment to homeschooling and their rejection of contemporary culture (a rejection not taken to the extreme of declining an invitation to appear on reality TV). Compare this with the tokenism of "born-again Christian" Harriet Hayes on NBC's dramedy *Studio 60 on the Sunset Strip*. Harriet's but a cipher, a rhetorical backboard against which ex-boyfriend Matt Albie can thwack his heathen wisecracks.

The competitions and elimination shows are latter-day Milgram experiments [scientific experiments in which participants are instructed to perform acts that conflict with their values] that place real people in artificial situations to *see what happens*. *The Apprentice* is Darwinism set loose inside an entrepreneurial Habitrail. Post-9/11, *Survivor* became less a fantasy and more a metaphor for an imagined postapocalyptic future. What happens on these shows might be a Technicolor version of how we behave in real life, but so is most fiction. Creative endeavors—written, scripted, or produced—should be measured not by how literally they replicate actual life but by how effectively they render emotional truths. The best moments found on reality TV are unscriptable, or beyond the grasp of most scriptwriters. It's no coincidence that 2006's best scripted dramas—*The Wire*, HBO's multi-season epic of inner-city Baltimore; and *Children of Men*, Alfonso Cuarón's futuristic thriller—were studies in meticulously crafted "realness," deploying naturalistic dialogue, decentered and chaotic action, stutter-step pacing, and a reporter's eye for the telling detail. *The Wire*'s season and Cuarón's movie both ended on semi-resolved novelistic notes, scorning the tendency in current television and cinema toward easy narrative closure. Watching them only threw into higher relief the inability of so much other scripted product to get beyond stock characterizations and pat narrative.

Contributing to the Documentary Boom

For all the snobbism in the doc community, reality TV has actually contributed to the recent boom in documentary filmmaking. The most successful docs of recent vintage have broken through in part by drawing heavily from reality television's bag of tricks, dropping the form's canonical insistence on pure observation. In *Fahrenheit 9/11*, Michael Moore brings an Army recruiter with him to confront legislators and urge them to enlist their children in the Iraq War effort. In *Bowling for Columbine*, Moore takes children who were shot at Columbine to a Kmart, where they ask for a refund on the bullets that are still lodged in their bodies. Of course, Moore's never been a doc purist. *TV Nation*, his short-lived 1994 television series, prefigured a long line of gonzo reality, from *Joe Millionaire* to *Punk'd*. Having the Serbian ambassador sing along to the Barney theme song ("I love you, you love me") while statistics about the number of Bosnians killed during the breakup of Yugoslavia appeared on the screen was not only ur-reality; it was ur-Borat. And speaking of talking animals, *March of the Penguins* turned stunning footage of mating and migrating penguins into an utterly contrived Antarctic version of *Love Story*.

The resistance to reality TV ultimately comes down to snobbery, usually of the generational variety. People under 30, in my experience, tend to embrace this programming; they're happy to be entertained, never mind the purity of conception. As an unapologetic producer of reality shows, I'm obviously biased, but I also know that any genre that provokes such howls of protest is doing something interesting. Try the crab.

> "The influence of Reality TV has been insidious, pervasive. It has ruined television, and by ruining television it has ruined America."

Reality Television Has No Value

James Wolcott

In the viewpoint that follows, Vanity Fair *contributing editor James Wolcott asserts that reality television has debased any artistic pretensions of television. In his opinion, reality television exploits viewers' desires to feel superior to those who parade themselves on the host of shows now prevalent on nearly every network. Wolcott argues that these "real life" celebrities at best cater to the audience's voyeuristic tendencies and at worst publicize racist attitudes, reinforce gender stereotypes, and display disturbing antisocial behaviors to millions of viewers each day. Wolcott worries that reality television programming has taken over the airwaves, discouraging producers from pursuing quality shows that have some intellectual merit.*

As you read, consider the following questions:

1. Why does Wolcott exclude competition reality shows from his fiery critique?

2. In what way have the A&E and Bravo networks changed their formatting in recent years, according to Wolcott?

3. As Wolcott reports, how did Karee Gibson Hart justify her "threatening antics" on the reality show *Bridezillas*?

I was recently in a Duane Reade drugstore, having a Hamlet fit of temporizing over which moisturizer to choose, when the normal tedium pervading the aisles was suddenly rent by the ranting distress of a young woman in her early 20s, pacing around and fuming into her cell phone. She made no effort to muffle her foulmouthed monologue, treating everyone to a one-sided tale of backstabbing betrayal—"She pretended to be my friend and sh** all over me"—as mascara ran down her cheeks like raccoon tears. Judging from the unanimous round of stony expressions from customers and cashiers alike, her *cri de coeur* [literally: cry from the heart] engendered no sympathy from the jury pool, partly because there was something phony about her angst, something "performative," as they say in cultural studies. Her meltdown was reminding me of something, and then it flashed: this is how drama queens behave on Reality TV—a perfect mimicry of every spoiled snot licensed to pout on Bravo or VH1 or MTV. The thin-skinned, martyred pride, the petulant, self-centered psychodrama—she was playing the scene as if a camera crew were present, recording her wailing solo for the highlight reel. Proof, perhaps, that the ruinous effects of Reality TV have reached street level and invaded the behavioral bloodstream, goading attention junkies to act as if we're all extras in their vanity production. There was a time when idealistic folksingers such as myself believed that Reality TV was a programming vogue that would peak and recede, leaving only its hardiest show-offs. Instead, it has metastasized like toxic mold, filling every nook and opening new crannies. *Idiocracy*, Mike Judge's satire about a future society too dumb to wipe itself, now looks like a prescient documentary.

I'm not talking about competition shows where actual talent undergoes stress tests as creative imagination and problem solving enter a field of play—elimination contests such as *Project Runway*, *Top Chef*, and, for all its sob-sisterhood, *America's Next Top Model*. It's the series that clog the neural pathways of pop culture with the contrived antics of glorified nobodies and semi-cherished has-beens that may help pave the yellow brick road for Sarah Palin, *Idiocracy*'s warrior queen. It is a genre that has foisted upon us Dog the Bounty Hunter, with his racist mouth and Rapunzel mullet; tricked-out posses of *Dynasty*-throwback vamps and nail-salon addicts (*The Real Housewives of Atlanta*, et al., the stars of which pose in the promos in tight skirts and twin-torpedo tops like lamppost hookers auditioning for *Irma la Douce*); and endless replays of Rodney King throwing up on *Celebrity Rehab with Dr. Drew*. The influence of Reality TV has been insidious, pervasive. It has ruined television, and by ruining television it has ruined America. Maybe America was already ruined, but if so, it's now even more ruined. Let us itemize the crop damage.

Lowering Network Property Values

On his weekly blog, author James Howard Kunstler (*The Long Emergency*) noted the significance of a memorial tribute to CBS news giant Walter Cronkite on *60 Minutes* being followed by "a childish and stupid 'reality' show called 'Big Brother,'" an Orwell-for-dummies exercise set in a hamster cage for preening narcissists where cameras surveil every calculated move. Kunstler observed, "This [scheduling] said even more about the craven quality of the people currently running CBS. It was also a useful lesson in the diminishing returns of technology as applied to television, since it should now be obvious that the expansion of cable broadcasting since the heyday of the 'big three' networks has led only to the mass replication of video garbage rather than a banquet of culture, as first touted." Not entirely so. Quality cable dramas such as *Nurse Jackie*, *The Wire*, *The Shield*, *Deadwood*, *The Sopranos*, *Breaking Bad*, and *Mad Men* have immeasurably enriched our petty lives, though there's really no excuse for *Californication*. But it is also true that the mega-dosage of reality programming has lowered the lowest common denominator to pre-literacy. Cable networks originally conceived as cultural alcoves, such as Bravo and A&E (Arts and Entertainment), abandoned any arty aspirations years ago and rebranded themselves as vanity mirrors for the upwardly mobile (Bravo) and police blotters for crime buffs (A&E). Pop music has been all but relegated to the remainder bin at MTV and VH1, where high-maintenance concoctions such as Paris Hilton, Flavor Flav, and Hulk Hogan's biohazard clan of bleached specimens provide endless hours of death-hastening diversion. Since reality programming is cheaper to produce than sitcoms or ensemble dramas (especially those requiring location shooting, which is why the *Law & Order* franchises spend less time on the streets, more time haunting the shadows of dimly lit sets), intricate brainteasers such as *Bones* (Fox), *Lost* (ABC), and the original *CSI* (CBS) have to fight even harder to hold their own against the plethora of reality shows catering to romantic fools looking to land a rich sucker—all those Bachelors and Bachelorettes sniffing red roses between tongue-wrestlings.

Annihilating the Classic Documentary

When was the last time you saw a prime-time documentary devoted to a serious subject worthy of Edward R. Murrow's smoke rings? Since never, that's when. They're extinct, relics of the prehistoric past, back when television pretended to espouse civic ideals. Murrow and his disciples have been supplanted by Jeff Probst, the grinny host of CBS's *Survivor*, framed by torchlight in some godforsaken place and addressing an assembly of coconuts.

Class Warfare and Proletarian Exploitation

While the queen bee of Reality TV, Bravo executive Lauren Zalaznick, is fawned over in a *New York Times Magazine* profile by Susan Dominus that elevates her into the Miranda Priestly [moviedom's devil who wore Prada] of the exegetical empyrean ("To her, what she's producing isn't rampant consumerism on display to be emulated or mocked, or both—it's a form of social anthropology, a cultural text as worthy of analysis as any other, an art form suitable for her intellect"), temporary serfdom is the lot of the peon drones being pushed to the breaking point. In an eye-opener published in *The New York Times* of August 2, [2009,] reporter Edward Wyatt revealed the sweatshop secrets of Reality TV's mini-stockades, where economic exploitation and psychological manipulation put the vise squeeze on contestants. "With no union representation, participants on reality series are not covered by Hollywood workplace rules governing meal breaks, minimum time off between shoots or even minimum wages," Wyatt wrote. "Most of them, in fact, receive little to no pay for their work." The migrant camera fodder is often kept isolated, sleep-deprived, and alcoholically louche [indecent] to render the subjects edgy and pliant and susceptible to fits. "If you combine no sleep with alcohol and no food, emotions are going to run high and people are going to be acting crazy," a former contestant on ABC's *The Bachelor* said. And crazy makes for good TV, whether it's Jeff Conaway unhinging on *Celebrity Rehab with Dr. Drew* ("911!") or some Bridezilla losing her precious sh** over a typo in the wedding invitation. One particularly awful Bridezilla, named Karee Gibson Hart, whose threatening antics may have violated her probation, defended herself by claiming she was simply "playing the game," putting on a diva act to show off her dramatic skills. Judge Judy might not buy that excuse, but there's no question that reality programs often resemble drama workshops for hapless amateurs, a charmless edition of *Waiting for Guffman*.

Reality TV Debases Bad Acting

Bad acting comes in many bags, various odors. It can be performed by cardboard refugees from an Ed Wood movie, reciting their dialogue off an eye chart, or by hopped-up pros looking to punch a hole through the fourth wall from pure ballistic force of personality, like Joe Pesci in a bad mood. I can respect bad acting that owns its own style. What I can't respect is bad acting that doesn't make an effort. In Andy Warhol's purgatorial version of home movies, those clinical studies of dermatology in action, his casts of beefcake/speed-freak/drag-queen exhibitionists had to work it for the camera, which kept rolling whether the objects of inspection were re-applying an eyelash or hogging the bathtub; his superstars had volumes of dead air to fill, no matter how near they were to nodding out. In John Cassavetes's cinéma vérité psychodramas, the actors were hot-wired for improvisation, encouraged to trust their ids and forage for raw truth stashed beneath the polite lies that make up our sham existence. These lancings of bourgeois convention weren't pretty, but they required sustained outbursts from the showboats involved, an expansive temperament. What kind of "acting" do we get from Reality TV? Eye-rollings. Dirty looks. Stick-figure Tinkertoy gestures. Incensed-mama head-waggings. Jaws dropped like drawbridges to convey stunned indignation.

Emotionally Emaciated

Nearly everyone conforms to crude, cartoon stereotype (bitch, gold digger, flamboyant gay, recovering addict, sofa spud, anal perfectionist, rageaholic), making as many pinched faces as the Botox will permit, a small-caliber barrage of reaction shots that can be cut from any random stretch of footage and pasted in later to punctuate an exchange. (Someone says something unconstructive—"That outfit makes her look like a load"—and *ping!* comes the reaction shot, indicating the poison dart has struck home.) Younger reality stars may have more mobile faces, though in time they too will acquire the Noh masks of the celebrity undead. Their range of verbal expression runs mostly from chirpy to duh, as if their primpy little mouths were texting. The chatty, petty ricochet of Reality TV—the he-said-that-you-said-that-she-said-that-I-said-that-she-said-that-your-fat-ass-can-no-longer-fit-through-the-door—eventually provokes a contrived climax, a "shock ending" that is tipped off in promos for the show, teasers replayed so frequently that it's as if the TV screen had the hiccups. The explosive payoff to the escalating sniper fire on *The Real Housewives of New Jersey* was a raging tantrum by Teresa Giudice, who flipped over a restaurant table in a She-Hulk fit of wrathful fury and called co-star Danielle Staub a "prostitution whore" (an interesting redundancy), all of which helped make for a unique dining experience and quite a season finale. Good manners and decorum are anathema to Reality TV, where impulsivity swings for the fences.

Rewarding Vulgar, Selfish, Antisocial Behavior

Ever since "Puck" put MTV's *Real World* on the map with his nose-picking, homophobic, rebel-without-a-clue posturings and earned notoriety as the first contestant to be evicted from the premises, self-centered jerkhood has put reality's lab rats on the publicity fast track. On Bravo's *Shear Genius*, Tabatha Coffey, doing a sawed-off version of Cruella De Vil, gloated with nasty delight after being eliminated from the show in a team challenge, because she was able to take a despised rival down with her; she exuded such Schadenfreude [taking pleasure in another's demise] that she made losing look like sweet victory, a sacrifice worth making to louse up someone else's chances. And what was the fallout from her unsporting, cold-dish behavior? Why, she received her own Bravo show—*Tabatha's Salon Takeover*, where she got to be a bossy boots, bestowing her bad attitude on the less fortunate. TLC's *Jon & Kate plus Eight* was a popular, wholesome family favorite, but it was a tacky act of alleged infidelity that turned the marital split of Jon and Kate Gosselin into a nova express, their un-civil war splashed across checkout-magazine covers as America took sides, choosing between Jon, the philandering dope with the dazed expression, and Kate, the castrator with the choppy Posh Spice hair. We are now stuck with them for the foresee-able future, just as we are saddled with MTV's *The Hills*' Spen-cer Pratt, who has just brought out a book—which is prob-ably one more than he's ever actually read—in which he caddishly boasts about his bastardly behavior toward Lauren Conrad, exulting in the wet hisses he and his wife, Heidi Montag, receive as America's least-admired bobbleheads. From the New York *Daily News*: "He brags in the book that he made a point of telling every blog around that a sex tape of nemesis [and former *Hills* star] Lauren Conrad existed. Why? Because he could. He . . . says he wouldn't have personally attacked Conrad had she not been so darn nasty to his then-girlfriend Montag." He's now thumping his chest in triumph at having helped drive Conrad off the show. "'If I weren't me, I'd hate me,' he announces." I hate him and I've never even seen *The Hills*, which only testifies to Reality TV's phenomenal out-reach, its ability to annoy even the uninitiated.

The ego maneuvers of a Tabatha or Spencer are minor-league Machiavelli compared with the latest scar on Reality TV's record—the savage murder of former bikini model Jas-mine Fiore, whose mutilated body was jammed into a trunk and discovered in a Dumpster. The chief suspect was her former husband, a reality star named Ryan Alexander Jenkins, whose paltry claim to fame was his having been a contestant on the VH1 reality show *Megan Wants a Millionaire*, that ample contribution to humanity. (The Megan in want of a millionaire is Megan Hauserman, a graduate of VH1's *Rock of Love: Charm School*, who aspires to the title of "trophy wife.") "The case cast an unsettling light on the casting practices of reality television, in particular the sometimes tawdry shows broadcast by VH1," reported Brian Stelter, in a *New York Times* story headlined, with a delicate understatement bordering on self-parody, KILLING RAISES NEW REALITY TV CONCERNS. Proper vetting would have revealed that Jenkins had been previously convicted of assault against a woman and would perhaps have disqualified him from appearing on *Megan Wants a Millionaire* and *I Love Money 3* (also VH1). Nine days after Fiore's disappearance, Jenkins was found hanging dead in a motel room, his suicide completing the circle of misery, brutality, and fame-grubbing futility. In his final caper novel, *Get Real*, the late Donald Westlake had his woebegone protagonist Dortmunder and his gang cast in a Reality TV series that would have them plotting and executing a heist as a camera crew tagged along, borderline accomplices in crime. An ingenious story line, but *Get Real* may have been outdone and then some by the Brazilian series *Canal Livre*, whose host, Wallace Souza, is alleged to have commissioned a fistful of murders to bump off rivals in the drug trade and to ensure that his cameras would be the first on the scene for the buzzard feast (arriving so promptly that gun smoke was still streaming from one victim's body). Ordering a hit and then dining out on the corpse—talk about controlling supply and demand at both ends!

Reality TV Gives Voyeurism a Dirty Name

For film directors from Alfred Hitchcock to Andy Warhol to Brian De Palma to Sam Peckinpah (whose last film, *The Osterman Weekend*, was set in a house rigged with closed-circuit TV) to Michael Haneke (*Caché*), voyeurism has been one of the great self-reflexive themes in postwar cinema, James Stewart with his zoom lens in *Rear Window* being the primary stand-in for us, the audience, spying at life through a long-range gaze. In thrillers, the idle viewer becomes implicated, ensnared, in the drama unfolding and discovers that voyeurism is a two-way mirror: Raymond Burr, the watched, glares across the courtyard and meets Stewart's binocular gaze—*contact*. In the voyeurism of Reality TV, the viewer's passivity is kept intact, pampered and massaged and force-fed Chicken McNuggets of carefully edited snippets that permit him or her to sit in easy judgment and feel superior at watching familiar strangers make fools of themselves. Reality TV looks in only one direction: down.

Periodical Bibliography

The following articles have been selected to supplement the diverse views presented in this chapter.

Robert J. Bresler   "Lost Horizons," *USA Today* (magazine), November 2009.

Mark Fisher   "The Age of Consent," *New Statesman*, December 14, 2009.

Nancy Franklin   "Jersey Jetsam," *New Yorker*, January 18, 2010.

Kara Jesella   "Cyberhood Is Powerful," *Ms.*, Summer 2009.

John Jurgensen   "Songs with Something to Say," *Wall Street Journal*, May 30, 2008.

James Poniewozik   ". . . But We Know What We Like," *Time*, April 16, 2007.

Alissa Quart   "Lost Media, Found Media," *Columbia Journalism Review*, May–June 2008.

Charles Soukup   "I Love the 80s: The Pleasures of a Postmodern History," *Southern Communication Journal*, January 2010.

Andrew Sullivan   "Why I Blog," *Atlantic Monthly*, November 2008.

CHAPTER 2

How Has the Internet Impacted Popular Culture?

Chapter Preface

The Internet has connected millions of people around the world and has immeasurably increased the speed at which information can be shared. Whereas once this technology was limited to computers, it now is available on cell phones, personal music players, and other handheld gadgets. The portability and relative inexpensiveness of this technology has made instant communication and the creation of Internet identities widely popular—especially among young people. In fact, for many adolescents in wealthy countries such as the United States, easy Internet access is commonplace, and this ubiquity has bred a new form of social networking.

Not everyone admires the Internet-based culture arising among today's youth, however. Joseph W. Gauld, the founder of Hyde Boarding Schools in Maine, penned a 2009 article in *Education Week* in which he expressed his concerns that "iCulture" is supplanting the family as the teacher of values to young people. He maintains that Internet social networking distances peers from each other and also fosters self-centeredness and elitism—attitudes that stifle meaningful relationships and undermine authority. Gauld points out that it is ironic that parents, whose authority he claims is eroding through the development of iCulture, end up providing their children with the latest technology for fear that their sons and daughters will be left behind or left out without it. "The shrinking influence of the American family and the loss of its support system—extended family, neighborhood, church, community, and other endangered face-to-face institutions—leave no counter to this highly organized iCulture," Gauld complains, and parents and children alike are perpetuating it at the expense of human interaction, he argues.

Gauld's opinion is shared by many critics who sense a radical shift in the way people communicate in the Internet age. Indeed, the Internet has changed the manner in which young and old envision relationships as well as personal identity. However, not everyone believes the Internet and social networking sites are a detriment to these facets of human interaction. Sarah Lacy, a writer for TechCrunch, a Weblog that analyzes the Internet's impact on business and society, asserts that networking Web sites such as Facebook and communication services such as Twitter provide young people with new tools to express themselves. She claims that these outlets "are more about extending your real identity and relationships online. That's what makes them so addictive: The little endorphin rushes from reconnecting with an old friend, the ability to passively stay in touch with people you care about but don't have the time to call every day." In Lacy's view, social networking sites and the like are very human and subject to the same social pressures that influence face-to-face relationships. She goes on to advocate that such forms of communication even enable people to keep in touch more often than do traditional communications systems.

Whether the Internet aids or hinders interpersonal relations will continue to be hotly debated as the new medium is still formatively extending its reach. In the following chapter, critics and analysts share their opinions about the Internet's influence on the way people interact and discuss the distinctions between the virtual and the real worlds.

> "When Internet TV becomes dramatically, unequivocally, and inexorably cheaper than the other three distribution models [broadcast, cable, and satellite], those other models will quickly go away."

Internet Television Will Replace Cable Television

Bob X. Cringely

Following the advent and popularization of the online video-viewing Web site YouTube, the debate about the future of television in the Internet age commenced. The recent introduction of streaming video Web sites, such as Hulu.com and TV.com, has further fueled arguments by those contending that the demise of traditional television providers is imminent. Bob X. Cringely advances this position in the following viewpoint and argues that television eventually will be broadcast solely by Internet service providers because the television providers that have to this point dominated the airwaves will no longer be able to offer the same quality of service at a competitive rate. Further, he predicts that the television content providers will occupy positions of greater importance, selling programs to the highest bidder or ablest broadcaster, which could be an entity such as Apple or Google. Bob X. Cringely is an author and computer technology consult-ant who previously wrote for InfoWorld *and has continued to contribute writings on technological advances to publications such as the* New York Times, Newsweek, *and* Forbes.

As you read, consider the following questions:

1. What are the four models for "live entertainment video distribution" identified by the author?

2. As stated by Cringely, what is the "important lesson" to learn when analyzing the four broadcast models, and what does this mean for Internet TV?

3. According to the author, when will the crossover to In-ternet TV occur?

My last column generated a lively debate on the prospects for various business and technical options for the deliv-ery of Internet TV so it makes sense to continue this topic and build it into a more full-featured model. I used to write quite a bit about this back when I was trying to get NerdTV going. The core of what I'll write here can be found in a couple dozen columns from back then. . . . You see the future of television IS Internet television. There is no other in sight.

No business or technology exists in a vacuum. They all have customers, users, competitors, and make use of resources in an environment that is not one of total abundance. This means that if there is going to be something like television in the future it is going to adapt to the distribution model that offers the highest price/performance, which is to say the high-est performance for the lowest cost. That is not how one would traditionally describe the Internet, but then times are changing.

The Four Models of Video Distribution

Whatever country you live in there are generally four models for live entertainment video distribution—broadcast, cable, satellite, and Internet.

Broadcast is a limited local resource and therefore more highly regulated than the others but it has traditionally featured the lowest cost per marginal user. That means it costs a lot to build and maintain a TV station but additional viewers within the service area can be added pretty much for free.

Cable offers more channel capacity than does broadcast but requires building a distribution network that's fairly expensive. While one could imagine a cable TV "station," the way the industry has grown is through cable operators becoming content aggregators offering many services over their expensive networks. That's the most efficient way for cable companies to serve the broadest audience and the only way that enables them to sell extra-cost services like pay-per-view, premium movie channels or, indeed, Internet service. Remember, though, that cable operators pay for nearly all of the content they carry, which is different from broadcast, where a lot of content is free to the broadcaster and some content even comes with money attached.

Satellite operators pay for their content, too. Satellite initially used wireless technology to offer cable content in rural areas where it was too expensive to build a wired network. Having gained economies of scale in the rural markets cable couldn't compete for, satellite has come to town competing generally on price. But satellite offers no practical Internet service. I know there are some and I tried one years ago (Starband) but they don't work well.

Internet TV is different from all these others. It began as a parasite on telephone and cable networks so the cost of building the network generally wasn't there, having already been covered for the most part by those earlier services. Internet TV is less of a network than a conduit; at present the Internet

Service Providers [ISPs] don't pay for video content but then neither do they get paid for it. Yet this common career attribute also makes Internet service often more profitable for telcos [telecommunications companies]and cable companies than the core services those companies were established to provide. Whatever you pay for Internet service, it is mainly profit for your ISP.

Service Improves and Cost Decreases

The important lesson to learn when it comes to these competitive services is that the first three—broadcast, cable, and satellite—are all going up in cost to their providers while the cost of providing Internet service is going down. In the USA, broadcast viewership is dropping, which means the cost per viewer is rising. Same for cable where viewers are stagnant, viewership is declining (number of hours of viewing) and the cost of content is rising. Satellite has been growing marginally but that could end at any moment and it shares the same content cost increases as cable. Meanwhile Internet service just gets faster and cheaper thanks to a Moore's Law[1] double whammy.

Remember Moore's Law works in two ways. It makes digital products ever cheaper AND ever more powerful. This has profound meaning for Internet TV because it continually increases the bandwidth we can get for the same dollar while giving our devices the capability to do even more with the same bandwidth.

Here's an example. My primary Internet connection is an 8 megabit-per-second business cable line with a service level agreement and static IP [Internet protocol] addresses [a number used to identify a device within a computer network as host or interface and to determine a network address]. I pay

---

1. A term used to describe the computing hardware phenomenon characterized by the doubling of the number of transistors placed inexpensively on integrated circuit boards used in digital electronic devices.

more than you do but then I get more, too, though even my service is crap compared to what you can get in Japan, Korea, and much of Europe. My primary computer WAS a Mac Pro G5/1.6 circa 2004. I should have replaced the G5 a couple years ago, I know, but my kids are in private schools and I keep buying airplane parts. I finally replaced the G5 last week, though, with a dual-core Mac Mini 2.0. Both the old and new computers had four gigs of RAM. Though my Internet connection can easily carry one or more 1080p H.264 video streams, there is no way that old G5 (which cost me $1999 in 2004 dollars) could play it. It didn't do much better with 720p for that matter. But the $750 Mini (small drive but lots of RAM) can easily decode 1080p.

This is the trend, then: our available bandwidth will go up while our devices will become more powerful, making better use of the bandwidth. The result, as always with Moore's Law, is either better services or lower total cost or maybe a little of both.

The Inevitable Crossover to Internet TV

What this means for the future of television is that we're approaching a point where Internet service will equal and then be lower than the marginal per-viewer cost of the broadcast TV model. This crossover will inevitably happen with the only question being when. That's a function of bandwidth costs decreasing at 50 percent per year and processing power increasing at 50 percent per year. My calculations suggest the crossover will happen around 2015, which used to seem like a long time away but no longer does.

When Internet TV becomes dramatically, unequivocally, and inexorably cheaper than the other three distribution models, those other models will quickly go away. That's why I argued in PBS [Public Broadcasting Service] meetings to forget about spending $1.8 billion to upgrade local stations for digital TV and instead sell or lease that spectrum for commercial

Money-Saving Internet TV

You pay a hefty cable or satellite TV bill each month—but what do you get for that money? A lot of stations you don't watch, interspersed with a few you like, containing entertainment that you can also find on the Internet. In fact, between the Net and old-fashioned, over-the-air broadcasts, you may have little reason to keep spending money on extra stations.

Of course, dumping your cable or satellite TV setup has some potential drawbacks. For one thing, you might not get good over-the-air signals in your area. If your cable company also supplies your Internet access, dropping the cable means losing the discount for two services from one provider. And you'll have to make some up-front investments in your new setup before you can start saving money. But for a lot of people, those investments will be more profitable than stocks bought two years ago.

Lincoln Spector,
PC World, *October 2009.*

data use and throw the resulting $3 billion (lease revenue plus the $1.8 billion savings) into rebuilding the network solely as an Internet service.

Nobody listened.

So there is a cliff rapidly approaching for television. Five years from now local TV stations will have the same complaints that local newspapers have today as many of them go out of business. Cable TV operators will become ISPs, period. Phone companies will be ISPs, too, and analog voice service will be gone completely. The regulatory implications of these changes should be interesting.

The End of Television Networks

Who, then, will be the players in this future TV? For the most part they will be the content providers, which probably doesn't mean traditional networks. And the networks know this, by the way. Hulu.com [the joint venture of ABC, Fox, and NBC to offer streaming television on the Internet] isn't called NBC-FoxABC.com and TV.com [CBS's site to offer its programs online] isn't called cbs.com for a reason. Networks will go away.

But content will endure, bringing new value to *I Love Lucy* episodes and almost anything else people like to watch.

The TV networks are throwing their lot together. CBS chairman Sumner Redstone will come to his senses one day and merge tv.com into Hulu, I am sure. Their big competitors will be Google, Apple, and a player yet to be even *founded* (definitely NOT Yahoo OR Microsoft).

The Value of Content Will Increase

Google will differentiate itself as always through technology. Those shipping container data centers I first wrote about in 2005 exist not just because they are easy to stack inside big Google plants. Why bother with weatherproof containers if they are to be used exclusively indoors? Because they are even easier to put in the parking lot at the telephone company central office or at the cable company head-end, both of which will by then be strictly ISPs. Google will proxy content at every major ISP in America. And they'll do this because Google has no idea what people want to watch on TV, nor do they particularly care.

Apple, on the other hand, cares. . . . Apple will attempt to become the dominant content provider to the 20 percent of the market that spends 80 percent of the money, with margins high enough to use Google distribution and still come out ahead, leaving to [Google cofounders Larry] Page and [Sergey] Brin the 80 percent of content that generates 20 percent of revenue.

But wait, isn't Apple just a maker of hardware? Don't they do iTunes just to sell iPods?

No.

Apple is a software company that has traditionally packaged its software in attractive hardware boxes. The fact that any new Mac is essentially a Windows computer proves that. But price points have been eroding in every hardware category and will continue to do so. Microsoft right now makes more profit from every Windows PC than does the maker of that PC. Apple is not immune to this trend. So the company needs to find ways to sell more and more software.

Content is software. TV is software. And the great thing about entertainment is that it is software we can be induced under some circumstances to buy over and over again like those teenage girls who paid to see *Titanic* dozens of times.

> *"YouTube is largely parasitic on television; without television or cinema, we could not use YouTube to view our favourite* Blackadder *clips or U2 videos."*

YouTube Will Not Replace Television

Patrick West

While new streaming video sites created by the major television networks provide viewers with an alternative means to view their favorite television shows, commentators continue to ponder the effect YouTube, which has no affiliation with these networks, has and will continue to have on television viewership. In the viewpoint that follows, Patrick West argues that YouTube is not usurping television in popularity and that this site, and the Internet in general, largely rely on television and other forms of media for content. The author contends that without traditional forms of media, the Internet—and YouTube in particular— would be at a loss for content. Further, he maintains that You-Tube is not nearly as powerful as people would like to think, with the case in point being that when a school shooter posted his plans for massacre on the site the day prior to the violence, nobody took the video seriously. Patrick West is the TV reviewer for the Web site Spiked and a cultural blogger.

As you read, consider the following questions:

1. The author claims that concerns about YouTube's replacing television are as misplaced as what other "scare stories"?

2. As stated by West, what are some of the things that bloggers must be willing to do to make the displacement of traditional media sources by Internet sources a reality?

3. According to the author, how was the Finnish school shooter, Pekka-Eric Auvinen's YouTube declaration symbolic?

"Humanity is Overrated." This was the t-shirt slogan that Pekka-Eric Auvinen, the Finnish school murderer, bore on his YouTube "massacre manifesto" video that he posted only hours before killing eight people and then himself on Wednesday [November 7, 2007]. The reaction to the atrocity has told us three things we already know, or already assume: The Finns are rather gloomy people; teenagers are rather confused; and we live in misanthropic [human-hating] times. But it also poses a question that many people have already been pondering. Is YouTube really that powerful, and will it—as some have prognosticated—kill off television?

Typical Teenage Angst

First, the Finns. They rival only the Portuguese as Europe's unhappiest and most melancholy people. This is the country that produced Jean Sibelius, one of the greatest Romantic composers of the late nineteenth and early twentieth centuries, whose oeuvre [body of work] mainly consists of dark, brooding and wistful compositions that are widely perceived to correctly portray the Finnish mindset. And when the Finns aren't trying to kill themselves all the time (they have one of the highest suicide rates in the world), they are normally trying to drink themselves to death. My brother returned from Finland two years ago and remarked how the Finns are bigger drunkards than the English—and even the Scots. What's worse, they all had mullets.

Then there is teenage angst. "I am a cynical existentialist, antihuman humanist, antisocialist social Darwinist, realistic idealist and godlike atheist", said Pekka-Eric Auvinen on YouTube. "This is my war: one man war against humanity, governments and weak-minded masses of the world! HUMANITY IS OVERRATED! It's time to put SURVIVAL OF THE FITTEST back on tracks!"

Now, we've all been teenagers at one stage, and I suspect some of us would have empathised with these confused and contradictory ramblings back in our youths, having read a bit of [existentialist philosophers Friedrich] Nietzsche or [Albert] Camus, or having listened to [British New Wave band] The Cure. Auvinen is, like myself, an aficionado of thrash metal, so I can see where he's coming from. Thrash metal is strange in that its message is that it wants to change the world for the better, but simultaneously it sees humanity as a cancer on the planet. The band Napalm Death (who I once met in Brixton; very charming, softly-spoken lads) sung "Multinational Corporations/Genocide of the Starving Nations" (as if to infer that were there no multinational corporations, humanity's lot could be improved). Yet their first album, *Scum*, was an observation directed at humanity in general. Auvinen's actions suggest how the thrash-metal, teenage mindset has become the norm in today's Rousseauian [like French Enlightenment philosopher Jean-Jacques Rousseau] liberal-left mindset: "I love the idea of humanity, but I actually hate people in real life."

The Second-Most-Popular Video Site

Just over a year ago [in 2008], Hulu sold out its advertising inventory. And while still a nascent offering, that was a notable achievement in a world of Internet startups largely focused on capturing users before dollars. Not that the site lacks for viewers: Hulu has grown at a clip not anticipated even by its own backers. In February [2009], less than a year after launch, Hulu became the Internet's second-most-popular video site, trailing only YouTube according to [the media ratings company] Nielsen.

Hulu has taken the lead in forging a business model for legal long-form Internet video, a content area that didn't even exist as recently as three years ago. Originally dismissed by critics, including some at YouTube parent Google who referred to it as "Clown Co.," Hulu was derided as a flawed strategy, a digital outlet for old media that consumers had no interest in watching. But advertisers viewed its potential differently, with 200 marketers signing up with Hulu in the past year. That said, in recent months, the amount of unsold inventory given over to public-service ads has been equally visible.

The answer as to why that's been happening may lie in the amount of new supply that has come with the site's jump in viewers, combined with the glut of broadcast inventory during this economic downturn. After Hulu debuted its "Alien" ad with Alec Baldwin on the Super Bowl, for example, the site saw a rise of more than 40 percent in streams.

Noreen O'Leary,
Media Week, *May 25, 2009.*

The Parasitic Internet

And, finally, there is YouTube. There has been much "moral panic" (yet another one of those dreadful phrases bandied around) about YouTube, about how it is degrading our youth, and, among media commentators, how it is threatening the future of television, as young 'uns are increasingly deserting television in favour of this internet alternative.

But fears about YouTube displacing television are just as misplaced as scare stories about blogs or websites in general displacing print or television journalism. YouTube is largely parasitic on television; without television or cinema, we could not use YouTube to view our favourite *Blackadder* clips or U2 videos. And the Internet is entirely parasitic on the BBC, CNN, Fox, *The Times*, the *Guardian*, books, magazines, radio, etc. Without the real world, the blogosphere could not exist. (And I do write this in full knowledge that I am actually writing this on the Internet, and am ironically being a parasite myself.) There is so much rubbish written about the death of the print media and television journalism, to be allegedly replaced by cyberspace, but the fact is that until bloggers are themselves prepared to go to Basra, [a key city in the Iraq War] or interview leading politicians or actually attend Barcelona v Glasgow Rangers [soccer match]—in person—there will be no news to report on. A YouTube/blogging generation deprived of its sources will be as impotent as its equivalent Man In The Pub deprived of his copy of the [London] *Daily Mail*: silenced.

The real question in Britain, regarding downloads, is: Will this kill off the television licence fee [the annual fee charged to citizens in the United Kingdom who own a television, with one fee covering all the TVs in the household]? You can watch television programmes on your computer and your mobile phone now, so do you need a television anymore? The licence fee is one of the few remaining socialist anachronisms of the twentieth century—an iniquitous poll tax on the people who watch the most television: the poor. Unbelievably, there used to be a radio licence fee in this country until 1971, and finally it is about time the TV licence fee was abolished. The BBC has tested our patience for too long with its profligacy, and it can no longer be justified, what with dozens of channels on Freeview and hundreds on SkyPlus. Not to mention YouTube.

Television's Superiority over YouTube

Pekka-Eric Auvinen's declaration on this website was symbolic in so many different ways, both profound and prosaic, of a narcissistic, self-destructive society; of how our culture has seemingly embraced anti-humanist, teenage values; of the breakdown between those who make programmes and those who watch them; of the power of the Internet, and its simultaneous impotence (no one took heed of Auvinen's YouTube posting).

In the end, anyone who thinks YouTube will replace television is misguided. Show me grainy coverage of one lame idiot falling into a river on that website and I'll show you footage from *Jackass* or *Dirty Sanchez* that is a hundred times funnier. And where did you think that footage of Filipino prisoners dancing to 'Radio Ga Ga' and 'Thriller' comes from? Yep, TV. And as for footage of some homicidal loser from Finland? I think I'll stick to Film 4 re-runs of *Reservoir Dogs* or *Goodfellas*.

> "The best thing about YouTube is that it
> has become the people's video library: a
> video Wikipedia."

YouTube Is Beneficial
to Society

Mick O'Leary

*In the following viewpoint, Mick O'Leary defends the value of
YouTube, arguing that it provides many benefits to modern society. O'Leary cites examples of the Web site's impact on political
races, enhancement of individual creativity, and its ability to
provide users with a means to discover new and interesting content related to their original search query. Mick O'Leary is the
director of Frederick Community College in Frederick, Mary-
land, and a regular contributor to* Information Today.

As you read, consider the following questions:

1. According to O'Leary, how many people watched and
   what was the result of the YouTube posting of the racially insensitive comments made by Virginia senate candidate George Allen?

2. As the author explains, what are some of the "descrip-
   tive data" included along with each YouTube video?

Mick O'Leary, "I Love YouTube," *Information Today*, vol. 25, December 2008, pp. 33–39.
Copyright © 2008 Information Today, Inc. Reproduced by permission.

3. What action does O'Leary report that YouTube members can take if they find the content of a video objectionable?

I love YouTube. Every video in the world is on there. Well, at least videos on everything in the world are on there. It's easy to use; there's no annoying computer back talk about "unsupported file type." And everybody else loves YouTube. It's the world's third most-popular website (Alexa ranking). Last July [2007], people viewed 5 billion YouTube videos.

But some people are always complaining about YouTube. They gripe that it's full of stupid people doing stupid things. They say it's an "anything goes" cesspool, full of pornography and other filth. They whine incessantly about copyright violations. As a YouTube lover, I'll respond to all of these complaints, and I won't duck the hardballs, unlike everyone else in today's public arena.

The People's Video Library

So you complain about guys hitting each other on the head? Who says this isn't art? Look at the Three Stooges, they were comedic geniuses. And what's your standard? Television with [talk show host] Jerry Springer and [reality weight-loss show] *The Biggest Loser*? Radio with [conservative hosts] Rush Limbaugh and Michael Savage? And you snobbish, elitist book readers are the worst. Look what's on your best-seller lists: *The Secret* [a book about self-help and spirituality] and *The Obama Nation* [a book containing factual errors about President Barack Obama].

No, YouTube is the people's favorite. Can you identify lonelygirl15, Judson Laipply, Kimbo Slice, Obama Girl, and Soulja Boy? No? Then you're the one who is out of it. They are all YouTube heroes. More people have viewed "Evolution of Dance" [created by Judson Laipply] than have read books in the last 5 years.

So you think YouTube's content comes from brain-dead slackers with body piercings and no jobs? Well, you're wrong. YouTube has lots of serious stuff. This [the 2008] is the most crucial election in recent memory, and YouTube has a video record of the entire campaign, from the presidential debates to candidate speeches in Iowa. A Democratic debate in July 2007 took questions from YouTube, and those were better than the softballs thrown by the big media moderators of the main debates. And people are watching this stuff. The notorious "Macaca" video from Virginia Sen. George Allen's campaign [in which the senator singled out a volunteer of Indian descent from his opponent's campaign using what many saw as racially charged comments] had 360,000 views on YouTube. It basically destroyed Allen's campaign (which YouTube deserves a public service award for doing).

If you like highbrow stuff, YouTube is a distribution channel for National Geographic, CSPAN, Reuters, and other earnest content producers. And it's not just recent material. Both commercial distributors and ordinary folks have added videos from the beginning of the medium: a unique and priceless historical and cultural record.

The best thing about YouTube is that it has become the people's video library: a video Wikipedia. Each of these wonderful creations shows the iceberg effect: You see a small part of the content on the surface (especially the loony stuff that attracts attention), while a much larger and more worthy mass remains below. In YouTube's case, it's many thousands of informative, entertaining, and sometimes unique videos. Through the conscientious work of thousands of dedicated YouTube viewers, this great treasure is available free to everyone.

A Complex and Comprehensive Database

People say YouTube is a careless jumble of junky videos haphazardly stuck on the web. Wrong again. YouTube is a real da-

"Good Enough" Technology

[Digital technology company] Pure Digital released what it called the Flip Ultra in 2007. The stripped-down camcorder—like the Single Use Digital Camera—had lots of downsides. It captured relatively low-quality 640 x 480 footage at a time when Sony, Panasonic, and Canon were launching camcorders capable of recording in 1080 hi-def. It had a minuscule viewing screen, no color-adjustment features, and only the most rudimentary controls. It didn't even have an optical zoom. But it was small (slightly bigger than a pack of smokes), inexpensive ($150, compared with $800 for a midpriced Sony), and so simple to operate—from recording to uploading—that pretty much anyone could figure it out in roughly 6.7 seconds.

Within a few months, Pure Digital could barely keep up with orders. Customers found that the Flip was the perfect way to get homebrew videos onto the suddenly flourishing YouTube, and the camera became a megahit, selling more than 1 million units in its first year. Today—just two years later—the Flip Ultra and its subsequent revisions are the best-selling video cameras in the US, commanding 17 percent of the camcorder market. Sony and Canon are now scrambling to catch up.

Robert Capps, Wired, *September 2009.*

tabase with a complex record structure, organized content, and good search features. Consider the miracle of YouTube's basic technology; you "film" something on your $30 cell phone, and YouTube turns it into [the 1962 film epic] *Lawrence of Arabia.* Each video has lots of descriptive data, including detailed usage statistics, a provider profile, viewer rankings, and viewer comments (more on this later). My favorite record element is the Related Videos feature. When you select a video, YouTube displays a set of subject-related videos. It's fiendishly effective, so you find yourself spending hours going from one fascinating clip to another. If I drop into YouTube to check some small point, I rarely get away less than 1 hour later, and then only under duress.

YouTube has good browsing and searching capabilities with 15 broad subject channels, which also have fascinating statistics about usage and popularity. The most popular channel is music. Comedy is a distant second. The single most-viewed video is [Canadian pop star] Avril Lavigne's "Girlfriend," (more than 106 million views); music videos, mostly loaded by music companies, dominate the top 10 list. YouTube has basic and advanced search modes, the latter with Boolean searching; field searching by channel, language, and length; and sorting by relevance, member rating, and view count. It even has cataloging in the form of provider-applied subject headings, known as "tags." This user-generated cataloging is quite effective and can be an acceptable—and even superior—alternative to formal cataloging systems. User tags are particularly useful at providing common, user-friendly search terms, which formal, fixed cataloging systems don't handle well.

Ongoing Complaints Are Unwarranted

Even fanatical YouTube viewers find something to complain about though. Google bought YouTube for $1.65 billion in 2006. The site itself had been launched only 1 year earlier, but the finances were troubling, despite its enormous popularity. The Google purchase brought a Midas-class parent into the deal. YouTubers were afraid that Google would slap on some uptight, politically correct shackles and ruin the fun, but that hasn't happened. Google brings in piles of cash and keeps the party going. What's not to like?

Then there's the copyright fuss. This tiresome complaint contends that YouTube is full of videos that violate copyright. Well, copyright is so 20th century. Negotiate a license and get over it. Viacom [parent company of MTV, BET, and Comedy Central and movie company Paramount] actually brought the biggest and angriest suit, but I have a solution: Google can buy Viacom and shut them up once and for all.

Other self-righteous types complain that YouTube has illicit content, especially pornography (I object to the John Hagee sermons [posted by the controversial, nondenominational pastor], but that's just me). Purely in the interest of journalistic responsibility, I have researched this topic, and yes, pornography exists on YouTube. However, it's blurry, soft-core, and that's no worse than what you'll see on cable TV.

And YouTube has specific guidelines for unacceptable content. Members can flag videos as objectionable, and then YouTube staffers examine the flagged items and may remove those videos in violation. So there aren't a lot of nasty YouTube videos, but member comments are another matter entirely. Those are full of ignorance, profanity, intolerance, and hate speech (including comments that the Aryan Brotherhood would censor), as well as heartbreaking punctuation abuse. Of course, none of this is any worse than what you'll see in blogs and reader comments all over the internet (a sound argument for retracting the First Amendment for internet speech).

Something for Everyone on YouTube

YouTube continues to add great material. "Evolution of Dance 2" appeared last June [2008]. Stupid-guy trick videos continue to be added. Tina Fey/Sarah Palin videos abound.

So all of you YouTube complainers: Relax and enjoy the wonderful world of Web 2.0. You old-schoolers can enjoy classic "music videos" of Tommy Dorsey, Duke Ellington, Count Basie, Louis Armstrong, Frank Sinatra, Hank Williams, Mahalia Jackson, and early Elvis. Meanwhile, I'll continue my search for illicit YouTube material and report back later (maybe).

> *"Twitter and other social networks skew young and tech-savvy, and as such provide a counterbalance to the one-way nature of the traditional media."*

Twitter Is a Catalyst for Meaningful Change

Sarah Jaffe

In 2006, Twitter founder Jack Dorsey launched the hybrid social networking, microblogging Web site. Users began posting updates of their daily and hourly activities. As a result of this constant connectedness, Twitter has been subjected to a range of criticism and praise. In the following viewpoint, Sarah Jaffe commends Twitter and argues that the site provides an opportunity for previously marginalized individuals to take a more active role in political activities, locally, nationally, and globally. Jaffe cites numerous examples of the organizing and advocacy power of Twitter to support her claims. Sarah Jaffe is a blogger, independent political journalist, and feminist pop culture critic whose work has been published in magazines such as the Nation, Bitch Magazine, *and* Bust.

As you read, consider the following questions:

1. After congressman Joe Wilson's outburst during President Barack Obama's speech about health care was publically criticized by Twitter users, how much money was Wilson's opponent in that year's election able to raise, according to Jaffe?

2. As stated by the author, how was the Media Equity Collaborative able to use Twitter to raise funds for scholarships to its national meeting?

3. Jaffe argues that Twitter action works best under what circumstances?

It was the shout heard 'round the world: During President Obama's healthcare speech to a joint session of Congress [in September 2009], Representative Joe Wilson of South Carolina erupted, yelling "You lie!" at the president.

The Internet exploded. Or more accurately, Twitter, the microblogging service that allows users to post 140-character "tweets" to a crowd of "followers," exploded. Twitter users watching the speech and commenting in real time were shocked and angered by Wilson's lack of respect, and almost immediately started circulating petitions calling for Wilson to apologize. A few tweeters (full disclosure: including me) shrugged off the idea of a petition and pointed out that the best way to get back at Wilson would be to donate money to his 2010 opponent, Democrat Rob Miller.

By September 15—a week after Wilson's outburst—Miller had raised over $1.5 million for his campaign. Bloggers picked up the call for donations to his campaign, but the action started on Twitter. With its immediacy and ability to spread information fast and far, Twitter takes "going viral" to a new level, and progressives like Miller are cleverly using its freewheeling nature to their advantage. The web tool derided by old-school commentators like [*New York Times* columnist]

Maureen Dowd as "a toy for bored celebrities and high-school girls" has come into its own; according to social-media monitor Mashable, as of September 2009 Twitter was the fastest-growing member community on the web—and, with a valuation of $1 billion, also one of the most flush.

User-Determined Information Streams

The rise of Twitter has met with plenty of resistance, as is the case with nearly all new media. The common complaint that no one cares what you had for breakfast misses the point; on Twitter, you choose whom to follow, whether it's for information or laughs. If someone constantly tweets banal details about her life, you don't follow her. You select your mix of friends, celebrities, bloggers, journalists, organizations, academics—anyone who provides you with information you want to know. Sure, you read some tweets that you don't care about, but you also get news you might otherwise have missed, and you get involved in action that you might never have heard about, even if that action is just to retweet to your own audience. Twitter lowers the barrier for participating in a debate or getting involved in a cause. People who don't usually discuss politics can retweet and spread the word, while people who live and breathe movements can find new compatriots via the digital world.

Rather than merely reinforcing existing social circles, Twitter networks are more like Venn diagrams: overlapping groups of people selecting whose tweets to receive. Information passes from group to group; people meet and converse and argue. You can click one link and see everyone who has addressed you, even if you choose not to follow them, and you can retweet a statement from someone you follow to those who follow you.

Marginalized Groups Use Twitter

The Media Equity Collaborative, an initiative to broaden funding for female-centered media, was having trouble raising funds for scholarships to its national meeting. But, using information she gleaned from Twitter, founder Ariel Dougherty secured funding from the Ms. Foundation. One day, Dougherty noticed that a few people she followed were in a meeting with the National Council for Research on Women, and followed links to discover that the Ms. Foundation's CEO was speaking to the meeting about the importance of building alliances with feminist organizations. "I seized the moment," she related, "and pounded off another e-mail to my contact at the Ms. Foundation."

Her request was granted, but, she noted, "Only because I was empowered with very timely information via Twitter was I inspired to act."

International Dialogue on Twitter

Many of the functions Twitter users count on were originally created by users. Hashtags—a word, abbreviation, or phrase squashed into one word, preceded by the # symbol, like #iranelection or #fem2—began as a way to highlight and spread specific information, and really opened the doors to activism on Twitter. The Twitter crew then modified the platform to accommodate their use, making hashtags clickable. (Clicking the tag sends you to a search window that lists everyone who has used that tag in their tweets, giving you a stream of information that users have determined is related to a single subject.)

During the upheaval in Iran immediately following the [2009] contested election, Iranians and supporters used the hashtag #iranelection to share info on demonstrations, news, and action in a country that had cracked down on the media, expelling foreign journalists and arresting local ones. Twitter became a sea of green—the color of the opposition party in Iran—as people changed their avatar colors in solidarity. Some changed their location to "Tehran" to make it harder for [incumbent Iranian president Mahmoud] Ahmadinejad's regime to locate the dissidents and close their connections. Users from around the world retweeted posts from Iranian tweeters and exchanged information on how to set up proxy servers for Iranians to use as the government shut them down.

For weeks, the #iranelection tag topped the "Trending Topics" sidebar, where the hottest topics on the service are shown as clickable links. Getting a topic to trend is the way to get the largest number of people to see it, since the sidebar appears on every Twitter user's home page, whether or not they have any interest in, say, Iran or "Pirate Day," the top trending topic as of this writing.

Trending topics shift rapidly, and new issues constantly rise to take the place of the old. British Twitterers, angry at the misrepresentation of their National Health Service in the U.S. media, created the hashtag #welovetheNHS and took over the Trending Topics sidebar for several days in August, just as the healthcare debate in the United States was reaching its boiling point.

Curious readers who clicked the #welovetheNHS topic were confronted with tweets from Brits sharing stories both poignant (@spoonbilledsand: #welovetheNHS I've lived with HIV for fifteen years and friends perished. NHS always did its best. Free and fair to all) and pithy (@JimmaeJames: #welovetheNHS i'd rather be taxed for a hospital bed than a bomb).

Influencing Corporate America

The #welovetheNHS hashtag had no specific action in mind, but another tag that flooded the Twitterverse recently aimed to—and did—change corporate policy. Back in April [2008], Amazon.com seemed to have removed the sales rankings from books that contained "adult" content. Mysteriously, adult content included feminism and LGBT [lesbian, gay, bisexual, and transgender] themes, while some outright porn maintained its rankings. Twitter went ballistic—#amazonfail was a top trending topic, and Twitterati like writer Neil Gaiman, who has more than a million followers, joined in the fray.

The #amazonfail happened on a weekend, and by Sunday evening Amazon had released a statement attributing the rankings' disappearance to a "glitch." Though some Twitterers responded with a new hashtag—#glitchmyass—the controversy died fairly quickly, considering the huge firestorm of protest and anger that was stirred up over the weekend. Yet one has to wonder if, without the Twitter outcry, the "glitch" would have been fixed so quickly, considering the targets were feminist and LGBT authors.

Though bloggers took up the cry—Jezebel [a blog for women about celebrity, sex, and fashion] listed books that lost their rankings—it was Twitter that really spread the word, fast and furious. Overlapping networks passed the latest news on quickly, and with it spread petitions and letters and blog posts from authors who found their work suddenly stripped of its rank and missing from search results. By Monday, most of the books had their rankings reinstated and Amazon had apologized.

The size of the outcry—and Amazon's response—was heartening. But Ahmadinejad is still in power, and the United States still doesn't have a healthcare reform law. Though people in Iran continue to fight, #iranelection is no longer forced onto everyone's radar by virtue of the sidebar, and #welovetheNHS is gone as well. Once a topic is no longer trending, it may not cease to exist, but for many it no longer matters.

The Limits of Twitter Calls to Action

And what if your topic doesn't trend? Blogger Heather "Dooce" Armstrong, who has more than 1.2 million followers, managed to get her brand-new washing machine fixed simply by complaining about it, by brand name, on Twitter. Yet most of us don't have a million Twitter followers. So how do we get our issues heard?

Twitter Encourages Innovation

In its short life, Twitter has been a hothouse of end-user innovation [in which the consumers of a product or service come up with new ways of using it to best suit their needs]: the hashtag; searching; its 11,000 third-party applications; all those creative new uses of Twitter—some of them banal, some of them spare and some of them sublime. Think about the community invention of the @ reply. It took a service that was essentially a series of isolated microbroadcasts, each individual tweet an island, and turned Twitter into a truly conversational medium. All of these adoptions create new kinds of value in the wider economy, and none of them actually originated at Twitter HQ. You don't need patents or Ph.D.s to build on this kind of platform.

This is what I ultimately find most inspiring about the Twitter phenomenon. We are living through the worst economic crisis in generations, with apocalyptic headlines threatening the end of capitalism as we know it, and yet in the middle of this chaos, the engineers at Twitter headquarters are scrambling to keep the servers up, application developers are releasing their latest builds, and ordinary users are figuring out all the ingenious ways to put these tools to use. There's a kind of resilience here that is worth savoring. The weather reports keep announcing that the sky is falling, but here we are—millions of us—sitting around trying to invent new ways to talk to one another.

Steven Johnson,
Time, *June 15, 2009.*

Dr. Susan Jacobson, of Temple University's School of Communications, said, "One of the golden rules of social networking is that thou shalt not inflict spam on your followers. So if you have a very pointed specific thing at a specific time, you can accomplish something." Jacobson pointed out that issues like the "100 Uniforms in 100 Hours" social media campaign to buy uniforms for Philadelphia public-school students had a specific objective and a short time frame that made it easily catch on. The uniforms were cheap—$20 apiece—so donors could feel that they made a difference for a child at a low price. Organizers kept a live count of the number of uniforms purchased, keeping followers informed of the action's success.

Twitter action seems to work best when it's spontaneous— the most rapid of rapid-response tools. When journalist Sarah Posner spotted a MediaBistro tweet noting that male journalists had three times the Twitter followers that female journalists did, she created a quick hashtag to rectify that: #followwomenjournas. Though the topic didn't make it to the Trending Topics sidebar, it did spread across the feminist and progressive Twit-o-spheres and female journalists connected and gained new followers, broadening the audience for their work.

Allyson Kapin used another Twitter action tool, act.ly, to achieve a similar goal. Kapin, the founder of Women Who Tech, used act.ly's petition tool to target Tim O'Reilly of the Web 2.0 summit and ask him to include more women on panels. Act.ly petitions are directed as responses to a particular user, flooding that person's response page with requests for action. Kapin later wrote on Fast Company's blog, "Was this an aggressive tactic? You bet. Did I get results? You bet. O'Reilly, bloggers, and other conference organizers responded immediately."

Voice of the Younger Generation

Twitter and other social networks skew young and tech-savvy, and as such provide a counterbalance to the one-way nature of the traditional media. For instance, over the past few decades, conservative voices have overwhelmingly dominated talk radio and now television, but the rise of the web opened up possibilities for cheaper, faster communication among underfunded progressive groups.

That's not to say conservatives don't use Twitter—#tcot, or top conservative on Twitter, is consistently popular. Like the radio noise machine, though, #tcot is consolidated. But like the left itself, the progressive movement on Twitter is less a bloc than a group of intersecting publics, each interested in a slightly different set of issues. When an issue or an event, such as Representative Wilson's outburst or the Amazon incident, captures the public's attention, Twitter is a forum for dialogue and multiple perspectives, helping progressives rapidly coalesce and respond.

Detractors of Twitter accuse it of being trendy, superficial, narcissistic, or just plain irritating. (Janelle Randazza, author of the new book *Go Tweet Yourself*, complains, among other things, "When was the last time you saw a tweet that 100 people needed to see? And, if 100 people did need to see it, wouldn't it have been a topic that required more than 140 characters' worth of information?") But the very aspects of the service that some find fault with—its young participants, its ever-changing onslaught of information—make Twitter a hotbed of social and political actions and connections. Will it eventually turn a profit? Maybe. Will Ashton Kutcher and other celebrity boosters soon move on to the next new thing? Almost definitely. But will Twitter, used productively, change the very face of civic engagement? That's the question that, while still unclear, is most compelling.

> "Using Twitter suggests a level of insecurity whereby, unless people recognise you, you cease to exist."

Twitter Is a Repository for Mundane Information

Andy Pemberton

In the viewpoint that follows, the author points out the short-comings of Twitter and argues that it is not the valuable communication tool that many of its proponents declare it to be. Andy Pemberton cites numerous psychologists who deplore Twitter as a medium that only exposes the narcissism, insecurity, and lack of identity in modern culture. Further, Pemberton delves into the reasons why individuals follow the tweets of celebrities and finds that the experts believe that Twitter followers want to be a part of something larger than their own world because they themselves are lost. Andy Pemberton is a British journalist.

As you read, consider the following questions:

1. According to the author, who is the most famous advocate of Twitter?

2. What are the various reasons people use Twitter, as described by Pemberton?

3. To what doting parent practice does Alain de Botton, as cited by the author, compare the use of Twitter?

"Arse, poo and widdle." With this unholy trinity of coy expletives, [British actor, comedian, and director] Stephen Fry introduced us to the joys of Twitter earlier this month [February 2009]. Fry was stuck in a lift [elevator] and posted a "tweet" about it. His naughty digital missive, together with a photo taken on a camera phone, put him at the vanguard of the latest social-networking phenomenon, which everyone from Hollywood to Wall Street is talking about.

Twitter's Exponential Growth

Launched in 2006, Twitter is the inescapable, hot tech product. It boasts 6m [6 million] users [as of February 2009]—teeny compared to Facebook's 150m—but its audience has surged by more than 1,000% in the past year. Twitter's most famous advocate is Barack Obama, whose Twitter account has 265,970 followers, more than anyone else. Fry is the second most followed tweeter, with 174,924; celebrities such as [British TV and radio personality and film critic] Jonathan Ross, [athletes] Shaquille O'Neal, Lance Armstrong, [actresses] Tina Fey and Lindsay Lohan trail behind. ("Jesus Christ" is listed as having 33 accounts, by the way, while "The Devil" has 189. [British biological theorist] "Richard Dawkins" has three.)

Right now, the San Francisco-based company that owns Twitter is valued at $250m, even though, in start-up argot, it is "pre-revenue". Its inventors, Biz Stone, 34—who describes Twitter communication as "like a flock of birds choreographed in flight"—and Evan Williams, 36, recently rejected an offer from Facebook to buy their company for $500m. Yet despite the big money and the enthusiasm swirling around his product, Williams (who also coined the term "blogger") has admitted many are bewildered when they first encounter Twitter. "We've heard time and time again: 'I really don't get it—why would anyone use it?'"

It's a fair question. What kind of person shares information with the world the minute they get it? And just who are the "followers" willing to tune into this rolling news service of the ego?

Twitter and Insecurity

The clinical psychologist Oliver James has his reservations. "Twittering stems from a lack of identity. It's a constant update of who you are, what you are, where you are. Nobody would Twitter if they had a strong sense of identity."

"We are the most narcissistic age ever," agrees Dr David Lewis, a cognitive neuropsychologist and director of research based at the University of Sussex. "Using Twitter suggests a level of insecurity whereby, unless people recognise you, you cease to exist. It may stave off insecurity in the short term, but it won't cure it."

For Alain de Botton, author of *Status Anxiety* and the forthcoming *The Pleasures and Sorrows of Work*, Twitter represents "a way of making sure you are permanently connected to somebody and somebody is permanently connected to you, proving that you are alive. It's like when a parent goes into a child's room to check the child is still breathing. It is a giant baby monitor."

Is that why tweets are often so breathtakingly mundane? Recently, the rock star John Mayer posted a tweet that read: "Looking for my Mosely Tribes sunglasses." Who wants to tell the world that? "The primary fantasy for most people is that we can be as connected as we were in the womb, a situation of total closeness," says de Botton. "When people who are very close are talking, they 'twitter away': 'It's a bit dusty here' or 'There's a squirrel in the garden.' They don't say, 'What do you think of Descartes's second treatise?' It doesn't matter what people say on their tweets—it's not the point."

The Need to Stay Connected and Relevant

"Tweets are really just a series of symbols," says Lewis. "The person writing it just wants to be in the forefront of your mind, nothing more." Which makes it very appealing to marketers. Companies such as Starbucks have been quick to recognise the marketing potential of Twitter, and makers of the critically acclaimed American TV show *Mad Men* received a profile bump when fans, posing as characters, sent tweets to one another. Even think tanks such as the Institute for Public Policy Research have begun using twitter to publicise their activities. It's not hard to understand why people might follow these tweets. But why do 174,924 people "follow" Fry's every thought?

"Receiving a tweet is like a friend whispering something in your ear," says de Botton. "We all want people to whisper secret messages to us. Children like to play 'I have a secret to tell you'. It's great fun, but what they say is often not very important."

"To 'follow' someone is to have a fantasy of who this person you're following is, and you use it as a map reference or signpost to guide your own life because you are lost," says James. "I would guess that the typical profile of a 'follower' is someone who is young and who feels marginalised, empty and pointless. They don't have an inner life," he says.

Jonathan Ross is a fan of Twitter for different reasons. He recently asked followers to nominate a word he could use in his Bafta [British Academy of Film and Television Arts, which hosts a yearly awards show somewhat like the Golden Globes in the United States] script. He went with "salad" and dropped it in 45 minutes into the show. For him, using new technology confers status.

"It makes us look young. And that is a high-status position in this society," says de Botton. "Perhaps closeness is not always possible, or desirable. Twitter gives us another option.

It says: I want to be in contact with you, but not too much. It's the equivalent of sending a postcard."

Periodical Bibliography

The following articles have been selected to supplement the diverse views presented in this chapter.

David Carr   "Why Twitter Will Endure," *New York Times*, January 3, 2010.

Simon Dumenco   "I Blame Twitter for the Fact That I Totally Hate Kittens," *Advertising Age*, October 12, 2009.

Steve Fox   "Internet TV: Almost Ready for Prime Time," *PC World*, May 2009.

David Glenn   "Arguments Heat Up over File Sharing and CD Sales," *Chronicle of Higher Education*, July 25, 2008.

Jefferson Graham   "Making It on YouTube," *USA Today*, December 16, 2009.

Ronald Grover   "Honest, Hollywood, Netflix Is Your Friend," *BusinessWeek*, January 11, 2010.

Ben Jones   "Governors Finding Tweets Sweet," *USA Today*, January 14, 2010.

Chuck Klosterman   "Anyone Seen My $4.2 Billion?" *Esquire*, April 2008.

Sujeet Mate and   "Mobile and Interactive Social Television," *IEEE*
Igor D.D. Curcio   *Communications Magazine*, December 2009.

Bill Persky   "We're Killing Communication," *USA Today*, November 2, 2009.

OPPOSING
VIEWPOINTS®
SERIES

CHAPTER 3

How Does Popular Culture Influence Society?

Chapter Preface

Researchers from the Prevention Research Center (PRC) of the Pacific Institute for Research and Evaluation in Berkeley, California, collected data from a pool of community college students aged fifteen to twenty-five and found that listening to rap music that mentioned violence or substance abuse increased the risk of these students abusing alcohol, using illicit drugs, and exhibiting aggressive behaviors. The study, published in 2006, concluded "that young people's substance use and aggressive behaviors may be related to their frequent exposure to music containing references to substance use and violence." The study, however, did not rule out the possibility that an unknown third factor might be responsible for the correlation.

The PRC study referenced previous research published in 1999 that determined that nearly half of all rap songs popular among adolescents mentioned alcohol use and almost two-thirds of these songs mentioned drug use. The PRC also cited earlier work that found rap videos to depict violence and guns more often than videos from other music genres. Coupled with other studies that showed connections between different varieties of music and aggressive and reckless behaviors, the PRC report asserted that "prior research suggests a connection between preferences for certain genres of music and alcohol and illicit-drug use, aggression, and other risky behaviors."

Despite such studies, critics charge that rap music—or any form of artistic expression—does not lure young people to bad behaviors but instead reflects the culture that surrounds the lives of many young people. Palm Beach, Florida, disc jockey Reggie Benoit told a newspaper investigating violence in the local rap community that "sometimes [rappers] talk about drugs because they have seen their parents die from drugs. Unfortunately, not everybody leads a good life and that's what the music is about." Other defenders of rap music have likewise insisted that rap musicians sing about violence because the urban environments where many of these performers grew up are plagued with gang warfare, drug deals gone bad, and police shootings. Rap musician Levell Crump (aka David Banner) testified before a 2007 congressional hearing on the issue, "I can admit that there are some problems in hip-hop, but it is only a reflection of what is taking place in our society. Hip-hop is sick because America is sick." Jeanita W. Richardson, a senior policy analyst for the State Council for Higher Education in Virginia, and Kim A. Scott, a professor of policy studies at Hofstra University in New York, supported this argument in a 2002 article for the *Journal of Negro Education*. "If there is in fact a culture of violence [in America]," the authors contend, "the true parent of rap lyrics is America herself, who financially rewards the glamorization of behaviors deemed socially unacceptable."

The debate concerning the supposed connection between music and public crises reveals just how influential popular culture has become. In the viewpoints that follow, experts and commentators debate whether other aspects of pop culture have made an impact on society and individual behaviors.

"A year of [violent video] game-playing likely contributes to making [children] more aggressive than they were when they started."

Violent Video Games Are Linked to Real-World Violence

Amanda Schaffer

In the following viewpoint, Amanda Schaffer, a staff writer for the Internet magazine Slate, *claims that research links playing violent video games to increased aggression in young people. Schaffer contends that numerous studies of various kinds establish this connection, and while none proves a causal relationship between video game violence and real-world violence, they do indicate that playing these games is a risk factor for young people to act out aggression in real-life situations. Schaffer maintains that better-targeted research is needed to pinpoint which games contribute to aggressive behavior and to identify what types of individuals might be more vulnerable to the violent content of these games.*

As you read, consider the following questions:

1. As Schaffer reports, what are the three types of studies that researchers use to connect video game violence to real-world violence?

2. As the author explains, what effects did researchers Craig Anderson and Karen Dill note in the outcome of the study they performed on 210 undergraduate students in 2000?

3. What "intuitive" connections does Schaffer say exist between violent video game content and increased levels of aggression in young people?

On *The Daily Show* on Thursday, April 26, [2007,] Jon Stewart made short work of the suggestion that the Virginia Tech shooter, Cho Seung-Hui, might have been influenced by violent video games. (Cho may or may not have played the popular first-person-shooter game *Counter-Strike* in high school.) A potential videogame connection has also been dangled after past killings, to the irritation of bloggers. The reports are that shooter Lee Boyd Malvo played the game Halo before his sniper attacks around Washington, D.C., and that Columbine killers Eric Harris and Dylan Klebold loved *Doom*. Does the link between video games and violence hold up?

Pathological acts of course have multiple, complex causes and are terribly hard to predict. And clearly, millions of people play *Counter-Strike, Halo*, and *Doom* and never commit crimes. But the subtler question is whether exposure to videogame violence is one risk factor for increased aggression: Is it associated with shifts in attitudes or responses that may predispose kids to act out? A large body of evidence suggests that this may be so. The studies have their shortcomings, but taken as a whole, they demonstrate that video games have a

potent impact on behavior and learning. Sorry, Jon Stewart, but you needn't be a fuddy-duddy to worry about the virtual worlds your child lives in.

The Methods of Measuring Aggression

Three kinds of research link violent video games to increased aggression. First, there are studies that look for correlations between exposure to these games and real-world aggression. This work suggests that kids who are more immersed in violent video games may be more likely to get into physical fights, argue with teachers, or display anger and hostility. Second, there is longitudinal research (measuring behavior over time) that assesses gaming habits and belligerence in a group of children. One example: A study of 430 third-, fourth-, and fifth-graders, published this year [2007] by psychologists Craig Anderson, Douglas Gentile, and Katherine Buckley, found that the kids who played more violent video games "changed over the school year to become more verbally aggressive, more physically aggressive," and less helpful to others.

Finally, experimental studies randomly assign subjects to play a violent or a nonviolent game, and then compare their levels of aggression. In work published in 2000, Anderson and Karen Dill randomly assigned 210 undergraduates to play *Wolfenstein 3-D*, a first-person-shooter game, or *Myst*, an adventure game in which players explore mazes and puzzles. Anderson and Dill found that when the students went on to play a second game, the *Wolfenstein 3-D* players were more likely to behave aggressively toward losing opponents. Given the chance to punish with blasts of noise, they chose to inflict significantly louder and longer blasts than the *Myst* kids did. Other recent work randomly assigned students to play violent or nonviolent games, and then analyzed differences in brain activation patterns using fMRI [functional magnetic resonance imaging] scans, but the research is so far difficult to assess.

Rehearsing Violence

Violent video games enable the player to identify with a violent character, which rehearses violent acts with much repetition. The player is rewarded by winning the game through numerous acts of violence. According to learning theory, the more-realistic experiences provided by interactive media may be more conducive to learning aggressive behavior than passive forms like TV and film.

Elizabeth K. Carll,
Chronicle of Higher Education, July 13, 2007.

Overwhelming Evidence

Each of these approaches has its flaws. The first kind of correlational study can never prove that video-game playing *causes* physical aggression. Maybe aggressive people are simply more apt to play violent games in the first place. Meanwhile, the randomized trials, like Anderson and Dill's, which do imply causation, necessarily depend on lab-based measures of aggression, such as whether subjects blast each other with noise. This is a respected measure, but obviously not the same as seeing whether real people hit or shoot each other. The longitudinal work, like this year's elementary-school study, is a useful middle ground: It shows that across the board, playing more-violent video games predicts higher levels of verbal and physical aggression later on. It doesn't matter why the kids started playing violent games or whether they were already more aggressive than their peers; the point is that a year of game-playing likely contributes to making them more aggressive than they were when they started. If we had only one of the three kinds of studies, the findings wouldn't mean much. But taken together, the body of research suggests a real connection.

Desensitizing Children to Violence

The connection between violent games and real violence is also fairly intuitive. In playing the games, kids are likely to become desensitized to gory images, which could make them less disturbing and perhaps easier to deal with in real life. The games may also encourage kids (and adults) to rehearse aggressive solutions to conflict, meaning that these thought processes may become more available to them when real-life conflicts arise, Anderson says. Video games also offer immediate feedback and constant small rewards—in the form of points, or access to new levels or weapons. And they tend to tailor tasks to a player's skill level, starting easy and getting harder. That makes them "phenomenal teachers," says Anderson, though "what they teach very much depends on content."

Critics counter that some kids may "use games to vent anger or distract themselves from problems," as psychiatry professor Cheryl Olson writes. This can be "functional" rather than unhealthy, depending on the kid's mental state and the extent of his game playing. But other studies suggest that venting anger doesn't reduce later aggressive behavior, so this thesis doesn't have the most solid support.

When video games aren't about violence, their capacity to teach can be a good thing. For patients suffering from arachnophobia, fear of flying, or post-traumatic stress disorder, therapists are beginning to use virtual realities as a desensitization tool. And despite the rap that they're a waste of time, video games may also teach visual attention and spatial skills. (Recently, a study showed that having played three or more hours of video games a week was a better predictor of a laparoscopic surgeon's skills than his or her level of surgical training.) The games also work for conveying information to kids that they will remember. Video games that teach diabetic kids how to take better care of themselves, for instance, were shown to decrease their diabetes-related urgent and emergency visits by 77 percent after six months.

Better Research Is Needed

Given all of this, it makes sense to be specific about which games may be linked to harmful effects and which to neutral or good ones. Better research is also needed to understand whether some kids are more vulnerable to video-game violence, and how exposure interacts with other risk factors for aggression like poverty, psychological disorders, and a history of abuse. Meanwhile, how about a game in which kids, shrinks, and late-night comics size up all these factors and help save the world?

| *"Video games say something about our culture; they don't make culture."*

Violent Video Games Are Not Linked to Real-World Violence

Torrey Meeks

Torrey Meeks is a staff writer for Blast *magazine, an online periodical that covers lifestyle and technology news. In the following viewpoint, Meeks claims that video games are simply the most recent scapegoat for a society that fears its own violent tendencies. As Meeks notes, statistics indicate that youth violence is declining, but social critics feel the need to pin tragic acts of violence—such as school shootings—on some facet of youth culture. Video games take the blame, in Meeks's opinion, because they are popular and they exhibit violent content. Meeks asserts that this is unfair because these games are reflections of the times, not shapers of culture at large. Meeks believes that society needs to examine real-world risk factors—such as the decay of urban centers and the pathological profiles of violent youth—before pointing a finger at video games.*

Torrey Meeks, "Study: Video Games Don't Cause Violence," *Blast*, April 1, 2007. Reproduced by permission.

As you read, consider the following questions:

1. As Meeks cites, what video game was demonized for supposedly contributing to the Columbine High School shooting in 1999?

2. According to Meeks, why was the video game *Missile Command* popular in the 1980s?

3. What does Meeks say stops him from "punching someone" after playing a violent video game such as *Grand Theft Auto: Vice City*?

In the last five years [2002–2007], video games have risen to prominence as the whipping boy of choice in the culture wars.

In the late 1980s and early 1990s, it was Hollywood. At that time, the movie industry was under increasing scrutiny due to violence on the big screen. Concerned politicians, at the behest of clamoring constituents, issued reprimands from the highest levels of government, castigating what they perceived to be irresponsible messages targeted at America's youth.

Around the mid-1990s, the explosive rise of rap and grunge—two music scenes mirroring the malcontent of youth from two completely different socio-economic backgrounds—stole the limelight, and it seemed that no matter what the new generation consumed by way of entertainment, nothing was safe.

A reactive message disseminated by conservative, religious authorities such as James Dobson, founder of the Christian fundamentalist group, Focus On The Family, was clear: The American way of life was under attack by irresponsible artists spewing messages of apathy, violence and anti-establishment rebellion.

With the exception of a troubling movement within the religious community, wherein some moderate sects gravitated towards more radical leaders, the attempts to bring the country as a whole back to what they saw as a more modest, sheltered, and morally upright lifestyle did little good.

Rock acts like Marilyn Manson, with in-your-face album titles like the divisive 1996 "Antichrist Superstar," were banned from performing in some cities, but to no effect; in many cases, it simply increased their notoriety and popularity. Rap icons like Dr. Dre, who pounded out tales of guns, drugs, money, and the hard-knock life of discrimination and poverty in the wealthiest nation on Earth, were demonized. Some went so far as to call him a latter day Lucifer. In the meantime, his albums smashed sales records, cementing his position in the celebrity firmament.

And Middle America worried.

Blame the Game

When the Columbine shootings exploded across the national consciousness like a hollow-point round [a particularly destructive bullet], it seemed that the jury was out. Rock music[ians] like Manson and rap stars like Dre rapidly went from contemptible—if harmless—diversions for middle class white kids, to the harbingers of ruin in a corrupt society on its last legs.

The mainstream press did little to quiet the post-Columbine media panic, highlighting the shooter's fixation with a new video game, radically different than its predecessors, *Doom*. The game, which today is rudimentary, for the first time incorporated stunning graphics, mass-market appeal and mind-boggling gore. Though it wasn't the first of its kind—the pioneering first-person shooter was arguably *Wolfenstein 3D*—suddenly, desperate parents had a fresh battleground from which to crusade against impropriety and misconduct, using the terrifying new medium as a rallying cry. Overnight, *Doom*—and video games as a whole—went from harmless entertainment to the missing link between otherwise 'well-adjusted' suburban youth, and acts of inexplicable, horrific violence.

At the time, little emphasis was placed on the shooter's underlying sociopathic tendencies, and in large part, that issue is still ignored. Those who found fault with video games rationalized that despite the mental unbalances present in the two shooters, without *Doom*, they would never have learned to commit such acts of cold-blooded homicide.

Almost seven years later, the verdict is still out. Violence, if anything, has increased in video games.

In less than five minutes, for example, I can turn on my television, stop a police car in the middle of the street, yank the officer out of his cruiser, and beat him to death with a golf club in front of unconcerned pedestrians.

The basic plot I just outlined is *Grand Theft Auto*, and it's far more advanced—both graphically and technologically—than *Doom*. And, since its release in 1998, has drawn its own hefty share of criticism not only from conservatives, but from liberals as well.

The debate centers around a vital question: Do violent video games create violent youth, or is violence in society—from isolated acts in the suburbs, to gang shootings at the decaying heart of a city—a problem that is far too complex to simply chalk up to an electronic sliver of the media machine?

Youth Violence Is Declining

According to the standard coffee shop rationale, an increase in violent video games does indeed prompt more violent youth. So it would stand to reason then that with the leaps in technology that have greased the skids on increasingly lifelike portrayals of gruesome death, our youth would be growing more violent statistically.

However, the opposite is true.

Sociologist Karen Sternheimer, specializing in pop culture and youth at the University of Southern California, and author of "It's Not the Media," and a recent article for the American Sociological Association, "Do Video Games Kill?" argues that blaming youth violence—suburban or urban—on video games is a gross over simplification of an incredibly tangled cultural skein.

Further, that based on numerous studies and statistical analyses, violent video games don't turn children into emotionless, trained killers.

"There are a lot of other issues that go on beyond the media explanation," said Sternheimer. "We're for some reason more interested in violence when it's committed by young people. But we didn't ask what kind of music and video games Tim McVeigh [the Oklahoma City bomber] was into. We kind [of] accepted this guy had some other issues going on, to say the least."

Her big picture stance flies in the face of what has, in the past few years, become pop culture dogma. In certain circles, when the subject of violence in the media and its impact on youth arises, it's taken at face value that the media is primarily to blame for what appears to be a disturbing trend.

However, the perception that youth are more violent today than they were ten years ago using high profile school shootings as a barometer, is not sound social science.

"High profile shootings allowed people to say see, violence is everywhere," said Sternheimer. "But something coverage of those shootings missed is that youth violence, in the same year that Columbine happened, was in decline. No one really noticed though, because those shootings are an emotional issue."

As stated in a report from the Surgeon General's office, "Youth Violence: A Report by the Surgeon General," in 2001,

Game Players Morally Responsible

Players of [*Grand Theft Auto IV*] can use the material at hand to revel in wanton violence and criminality, but they don't have to. People who haven't played the game often don't realise that in *GTA IV*, as in the real world, the purpose of a car, a driver, and a pedestrian can be a carjacking or a hit-and-run killing, but it can also be a taxi ride. This adds a moral dimension to the game. For Aristotle (and for most Westerners thereafter), to be morally responsible for something, you must have caused it and you must have been able to do otherwise. So, where *GTA IV* gives players an option to indulge in violence but does not compel them to do so, players are morally responsible for their wrongdoing.

Benjamin Hourigan,
Institute of Public Affairs Review, *July 2008.*

starting in the mid-1990s, "overall arrest rates began to decline, returning by 1999 to rates only slightly higher than those in 1983."

There is no disagreement among experts on both sides of the fence that the types of violence serious enough to garner police attention—with the exception of unreported rapes, which are resistant to statistical analysis—plummeted across the board, including school shootings.

Indeed, even in 1999, the year the Columbine shootings occurred, the trend in decreasing violent crime still experienced an overall statistical downturn.

And those were the prime years that violent video games came to the fore as a dominant form of entertainment. . . .

And here the issue arrives at something of an impasse. The numbers don't lie. Violent crime is down, but violence in video games is up. What role, then, do video games play in shaping the way we interact with the world? With enough focused exposure to violence in video games and other media, will our culture grow more violent despite the present statistical downturn?

Going from the solid foundation of numbers and scientific analysis to the philosophy of entertainment, video game historian Keith Feinstein, founder of Videotopia, the world's first comprehensive video game museum, having tracked the evolution of games from the first Pong console to the Playstation 3, doesn't think so.

"There are worse culprits than video games, and animated films are a great example," said Feinstein. "If it wasn't made by Pixar, you're hurting an animal for a laugh, or hurting someone for a laugh. There's a general crudeness, a general meanness that creeps into culture, and that has nothing to do with video games."

Elaborating further, Feinstein said that it's not so much the video game, or the violence itself, that is the issue at play in the culture wars. Moreover, it's the underlying technology that frightens older generations who can't comprehend the fast changing mechanics shaping the way the world interacts.

"People who were brought up on the Atari, a lot of them have dropped out of video game scene," said Feinstein. "They don't understand the modern language. They become frightened of what they don't understand."

And when people are frightened, oversimplifying a complex problem becomes attractive as a quick, easy fix to an otherwise imposing cultural barrier. In order to break the barrier down to its most basic building blocks, a few questions must be asked. Are video games an art form?

Video Games Reflect Culture

Feinstein says yes, unequivocally, they are. The story lines, graphical skill, and interaction of many different elements to make a product that is entertaining, beautiful, and meaningful classifies them as art.

Since video games are an art form, then does art influence culture, or does culture influence art?

The answer to that question, as in all things, can be found in moderation. According to Feinstein and Sternheimer, art forms are primarily a reflection of the world around us. However, art can influence culture.

Many times, it acts as a cultural catalyst, expressing ideas in a way that connects to an unrealized sub-current that ultimately rises to prominence due to the artists' giving voice to a generation's issues and needs.

"It brings a lens to things, and [Pablo] Picasso's work is great because of what it turned society on to," said Feinstein. "They were, frankly, a bunch of very elitist, super-educated, unsuccessful people. But they talked and they made a big difference in the world. It started an entire movement. Pieces of art can do that, and they can reflect culture in the same way."

Video games had the same impact in the 1980s. A small, groundbreaking game known as *Missile Command* was released on the Atari in the [President Ronald] Reagan era of nuclear proliferation. Armament was a paramount issue at the time, uniting the country across cultural divides. No one knew when, how, or why, but a significant portion of the population thought that on some scale, nuclear war was inevitable.

In *Missile Command*, nuclear missiles fell out of the sky. It was the job of the missile commander holding the controller to shoot the bombs from the air before they ruined the city. It started slow and picked up the pace with each new level, quickly reaching impossible speed.

"I was frightened to death back then, and *Missile Command* was a perfect reflection of that. It turned everyone's attention to the issue," said Feinstein. "[*Missile Command*] was featured in a whole bunch of movies and news programs. And the big lesson with the game? No matter what happens, you lose. Even with the highest score, you get the big blast because you can't keep up."

And while not all video games ultimately give voice to a generation—*PacMan* is today merely an iconic reference point—games do have the ability to influence culture and ideas. On that basis, video games say something about our culture; they don't make culture.

Grand Theft Auto, another popular game generations removed from *Missile Command*, reflects this sentiment.

"It's brilliantly designed, and completely morally reprehensible. That's what it is. So if you're looking to games to teach your children, you're making a very big mistake," said Feinstein. "If you don't want *Grand Theft Auto* in your house, don't have it in your house. Sure, your kids are probably going to go play it somewhere else: But it's not the medium or the message. It's how you're taught to interpret the message."

Personal Responsibility Is Needed

The problem is one of context and personal responsibility, more than video games creating killer kids. "Yeah," said Feinstein, "the Columbine shooters played with pipe bombs in their basement and no one stopped them from playing *Doom*. But no one stopped them from building pipe bombs in their basement, either."

Like it or not, soon people will be getting the majority of their entertainment needs from video games. For example, today, more people play NBA basketball games on console systems than attend live NBA basketball games. And that means, more than anything, it's a matter of choice. What will you consume, and how will you interpret the message?

Today, I find myself a ruthless mob boss after recently beating *Grand Theft Auto: Vice City*. I've sniped innocent pedestrians from rooftops and blown up exactly 160 stolen vehicles. Because I never drove a tank through the middle of the city and survived, I'm only at 80% completion for the game, according to handy statistics provided in order to gauge my criminality.

Yet I understand that going out onto the street and punching someone in the face will land me in prison, not to mention the penalties for hijacking an attack helicopter and strafing a police station. The consequences of such actions aren't savory, and I know that it is not a good way to live my life.

Still, I greatly enjoy the game, and this is because we all have violent tendencies, according to Feinstein. Video games reflect an inherent biological impulse. In our society, violence in any form is often seen as unhealthy; it is a thing to be suppressed, ignored, and ultimately, little talked about on a personal level.

But that sets a dangerous precedent.

"Who's to say violence is an unhealthy impulse? [Without it] we wouldn't be alive and we couldn't feed ourselves. We wouldn't have the culture we live in," said Feinstein. "We all have violent tendencies. If only a few people had violent tendencies, we'd all be enslaved. So I don't think violence is necessarily an evil thing. We are in a lot of ways animals that are ill adapted to the culture we've created for ourselves. So there are impulses that no longer fit into the society we have today, but that doesn't make them negative."

And in a society wherein real acts of violence don't fit into the going paradigm, video games may indeed help channel and redirect those self-same impulses, though there is much debate on that issue, and there is no conclusive scientific proof one way or the other.

| *"The principles on which video-game design is based are foundational to the kind of learning that enables children to become innovators and lifelong learners."* |

What Video Games Can Teach Us About Making Students Want to Learn

James Paul Gee

James Paul Gee argues in the following viewpoint that video games are excellent tools to teach children challenging cognitive skills. Gee claims that many video games require players to build characters and even worlds from scratch, engaging creativity and exemplifying the notion that each modification may lead to different game outcomes. Several of these types of video games teach children that in order to master specific feats or overcome obstacles, they will need to understand the complex relationships between their character, the character's skills, and the game situation. According to Gee, many players test various combinations of game elements to find out which options lead to the best re-

James Paul Gee, "The Classroom of Popular Culture: What Video Games Can Teach Us about Making Students Want to Learn," *Harvard Education Letter*, 21:6, November–December 2005, pp. 6–8. Copyright © by President and Fellows of Harvard College. All rights reserved. Excerpted with permission. For more information, please visit www.edletter.org.

sult. All of the mechanics and experimentation, Gee asserts, develop and exercise fairly high-order cognitive abilities in players and teach players to apply such principles in approaching real-world problems. James Paul Gee is a professor of reading at the University of Wisconsin–Madison. His field of study focuses on the intersection of language, literacy, and learning. He is the author of numerous articles and several books, including Sociolinguistics and Literacies *and* Situated Language and Learning.

As you read, consider the following questions:

1. How do the best video games create "an ongoing cycle of consolidation and challenge," in Gee's words?

2. What does the author mean when he writes that video games operate on the principle of "performance before competence"?

3. How does Gee define "smart tools" within video games?

Why is it that many children can't sit still long enough to finish their homework and yet will spend hours playing games on the computer? Video games are spectacularly successful at engaging young learners. It's not because they are easy. Good video games are long, complex, and difficult. They have to be; if they were dumbed down, no one would want to play. But if children couldn't figure out how to play them— and have fun doing so—game designers would soon go out of business.

To succeed, game designers incorporate principles of learning that are well supported by current research. Put simply, they recruit learning as a form of pleasure. Games like *Rise of Nations, Age of Mythology, Deus Ex, The Elder Scrolls III: Morrowind,* and *Tony Hawk's Underground* teach children not only how to play but how to learn, and to keep on learning.

Children have to learn long, complex, and difficult things in school, too. They need to be able to learn in deep ways: to improvise, innovate, and challenge themselves; to develop concepts, skills, and relationships that will allow them to explore new worlds; to experience learning as a source of enjoyment and as a way to explore and discover who they are. Let's look at how this kind of learning works in cutting-edge video games. We might learn something ourselves.

Players Are Producers, Not Consumers

To start with, good video games offer players strong identities. In some games, players learn to view the virtual world through the eyes of a distinctive personality, like the solitary Special Forces operative Solid Snake in the espionage action game *Metal Gear Solid*. In others, like the epic role-playing game *The Elder Scrolls III: Morrowind*, each player builds a character from the ground up and explores the game from that character's point of view. Game designers recognize that learning and identity are interrelated. Learning a new domain, whether physics or furniture-making, requires students to see the world in new ways—in the ways physicists or furniture-makers do.

Game designers let players be producers, not just consumers. Players codesign a game through their unique actions and decisions. Many games come with software that allows players to modify ("mod") them to produce new scenarios or whole new games. For instance, in the Tony Hawk skateboarding games, players can design their own skate parks. At another level, an open-ended game like *The Elder Scrolls III: Morrowind*, in which each character undertakes his or her own journey, ultimately becomes a different experience for each player.

Players can also customize games to fit their learning and playing styles, since well-designed games allow problems to be solved in multiple ways. For example, in the two *Deus Ex* games, many of the problems a player faces can be solved in at least three ways: using stealth, confrontation, or persuasion.

Virtual-World Accountability

When considering just how "real" anything that takes place in a virtual environment can be, it is, first of all, worth remembering the degree to which most real-life activities, from work to shopping to dating, demand a degree of self-concealment precisely because of the direct consequences they entail. A virtual world is a tremendous leveller in terms of wealth, age, appearance, ethnicity and the like—a crucial fact for anyone who isn't in the optimum social category of being, say, attractive and affluent and aged between 20 and 35. It's also a place where "you" are composed entirely of your words and actions: something that breeds within and around many games an often extraordinarily complex network of conventions and debates that are integral to a community held together only by voluntary bonds.

Tom Chatfield,
Observer (London), January 10, 2010.

Many games also offer levels of play for beginning, experienced, or advanced players, letting players choose the degree of challenge they are comfortable with. In some games, players can test their own skills. For example, the real-time strategy game *Rise of Nations* asks, "How fast can you get to the Gunpowder Age? Find out if your resource-management skills are good enough."

Features like these encourage players to take risks, explore, and try new things. If they fail, the consequences are minimal—they can start over from their last saved game. All these factors give players a real sense of agency, ownership, and control. It's their game.

A Cycle of Mastery

But learning goes yet deeper in well-designed games. Research has shown that when learners are left completely free to solve a complex problem, they may hit on creative solutions. But these solutions may not necessarily help them generate good hypotheses for solving later problems, even easier ones. A simple classroom example is the case of the young child who comes to think that reading means memorizing words. This may work perfectly well—until the child is swamped by the marked increase in vocabulary in more complex books.

In good video games problems are well ordered, so that early ones lead the player to formulate hypotheses that work well for solving later, harder problems. For example, if stealth is important in a game, the first levels will clearly show the player why confrontation is a less effective option, so as not to reinforce skills that will later undermine the player's success.

This well-ordered sequence creates an ongoing cycle of consolidation and challenge that enables players to confront an initial set of problems, and then practice solving them until they have routinized their mastery. The game then throws out a new class of problem, requiring players to come up with new solutions. This phase of mastery is consolidated through repetition, only to be challenged again. In this way, good games stay within, but at the outer edge of, the player's competence. They feel doable, but challenging. This makes them pleasantly frustrating, putting players in what psychologists call a "flow" state.

Video games operate on the principle of "performance before competence." That is, players can learn as they play, rather than having to master an entire body of knowledge before being able to put it to use. Research shows that students learn best when they learn in context—that is, when they can relate words, concepts, skills, or strategies to prior experience. In fact, many students are alienated from what they learn in school because those connections and experiences are absent.

Video games are simulations of new experiences and new worlds, yet they are able to engage players with languages and ways of thinking with which they have no prior experience. Players encounter new words and techniques in the context of play, not as abstract definitions or sets of rules. This holds their interest and spurs them on to develop new skills, vocabularies, relationships, and attitudes—irrespective of factors like race and class.

One way players can increase their competence is to seek advice from other players. There are websites and Internet chat rooms for almost any game, where players trade tips and stories, and where questions can be posted. Experts can help novices and peers can pool information. New knowledge is available just in time—when players need it—or on demand—when players ask for it.

Preparation for a Complex World

Finally, good video games nurture higher-order thinking skills. They encourage players to think in terms of relationships, not isolated events or facts. In a game like *Rise of Nations*, for example, players need to think about how each step they take might affect their future actions and the actions of their opponents as they try to advance their civilizations through the ages. These kinds of games encourage players to explore their options thoroughly rather than taking the straightest and swiftest path, and to reconceive their goals from time to time—good skills in a world full of complex, high-risk systems.

Video games teach players to capitalize on "smart tools," distributed knowledge, and cross-functional teams. The virtual characters one manipulates in a game are smart tools. They have skills and knowledge of their own, which they lend to the player. For example, the citizens in *Rise of Nations* know how to build cities, but the player needs to know where to build them. In multiplayer games like *World of WarCraft*, players form teams in which each player contributes a different set of skills. Each player must master a specialty, since a Mage plays differently than a Warrior, but the players must understand each other's specializations well enough to coordinate with one another. Thus, the knowledge needed to play the games is distributed among a set of real people and their smart tools, much as in a modern science lab or high-tech workplace.

In his bestselling book *The World Is Flat*, Thomas Friedman argues that the United States is facing a looming educational crisis. Even highly skilled jobs in radiology, computer science, or engineering are being outsourced to low-cost centers. Any job that involves standardized skills can be exported. To maintain their competitive advantage, workers in industrialized countries will need to go beyond a mastery of standardized skills to become flexible, adaptive, lifelong learners of new skills. Yet U.S. schools are focused more than ever on the "basics," measuring their success with standardized tests that assess standardized skills.

It is ironic that young people today are often exposed to more creative and challenging learning experiences in popular culture than they are in school. The principles on which video-game design is based are foundational to the kind of learning that enables children to become innovators and lifelong learners. Yet how many of today's classrooms actually incorporate these principles as thoroughly and deeply as these games do? Let's ask ourselves how we can make learning in or out of school more "game-like"—not in the sense of playing games in class, but by making the experience of learning as motivating, stimulating, collaborative, and rewarding as the experience of playing a well-designed video game.

> "Laboratory studies indicate that children exposed to a filmed sequence of violent acts frequently imitate those aggressive behaviors."

Television Violence Contributes to Aggressive Behavior in Young People

Deborah A. Fisher

Deborah A. Fisher is a research scientist and member of the Pacific Institute for Research and Evaluation, an organization that seeks to improve public health and safety. Fisher's studies focus on youth risk factors, and in the following viewpoint, she argues that television violence increases the likelihood of aggression in young people. According to Fisher, numerous studies have shown that watching violent programming desensitizes young viewers to violence and leads them to believe that violence is an acceptable response to interpersonal conflicts. Fisher penned this essay as the introduction to the Parents Television Council's 2007 report Dying to Entertain, *which tracked the number of violent acts committed on screen during prime time television broadcasts and discussed the impact on young viewers.*

Deborah A. Fisher, *Dying to Entertain: Violence on Prime Time Broadcast Television 1998–2006.* Alexandria, VA: Parents Television Council, 2007. Copyright © 2007 Parents Television Council. Reproduced by permission.

As you read, consider the following questions:

1. On average, how many murders, rapes, and assaults do young people see on television every year, according to Fisher?

2. As the author relates, what happens physiologically during the process of desensitization?

3. In Fisher's opinion, why is it problematic when television role models who use violence are perceived as attractive to young viewers?

Since its inception, adults have been concerned about the potential negative influences of television on children and adolescents, particularly through exposure to violent content. Foremost among the issues that have been raised is whether violence on television affects young people and, if so, how. Given that on average American youth witness more than 1,000 murders, rapes, and assaults per year on television, understanding the consequences of such exposure is an important public health issue.

Consistent Findings from Multiple Studies

The role of television violence in shaping young people's aggressive attitudes and behaviors has been studied extensively using a variety of research designs, and a body of consistent findings has emerged. Laboratory studies indicate that children exposed to a filmed sequence of violent acts frequently imitate those aggressive behaviors. Correlational studies of simultaneous exposure to televised violence and real world aggression have shown significant associations between the two behaviors. That is, the two behaviors tend to co-occur. The question of whether viewing television violence causes aggression, however, requires looking at which comes first. Does exposure to television violence precede aggression? The strongest evidence regarding the causal role of television violence comes from longitudinal studies involving data collected from participants at multiple points in time. Early exposure to television violence has consistently emerged as a significant predictor of later aggression in studies conducted in the United States as well as other countries, some of which have followed young people more than one to two decades beyond childhood.

In addition to aggressive attitudes and behaviors, research suggests that televised violence influences youth in other important ways. Viewing violent content is associated with intense emotional responses of fear and anxiety among both children and teenagers. Aside from distress and other immediate effects, such as obsessive thoughts and sleep disturbances, exposure to televised violence may also lead to an increased fear of being victimized. The power of violent portrayals to affect youth emotionally and psychologically is further supported by the finding that children frequently develop long-term fears of specific kinds of people or places from viewing a single movie or television scene that frightened them.

Desensitization to Violent Images

Finally, an important process known as desensitization has been linked to television violence. Desensitization occurs when an individual experiences a reduction in responsiveness to a stimulus—in this case, violence portrayals—as a result of repeated exposure. Desensitization to televised violence is evident on a physiological level through reduced arousal and emotional distress while witnessing violence. It also exists on an interpersonal level and is exhibited by less sympathy for the victims of violence and a decreased willingness to intervene in a conflict even if only to summon an adult for help.

Several characteristics of violence on television have been identified as contributing to its negative effects. For one thing, portrayals of violence tend to be presented as humorous rather than serious or realistic. Second, violence shown on television

Incidence of Violence Depicted on Prime Time (8 pm–11 pm) Broadcast Television between 2003 and 2006

Overall	2003–04 Violence (Per Hour)	% Change '04–'05	2004–05 Violence (Per Hour)	% Change '05–'06	2005–06 Violence (Per Hour)
ABC	4.20	64.5%▼	1.49	155.0%▲	3.80
CBS	4.60	6.5%▼	4.30	29.3%▲	5.56
Fox	5.32	2.3%▲	5.44	29.4%▼	3.84
NBC	1.89	95.8%▲	3.70	83.5%▲	6.79
UPN*	2.10	49.5%▼	1.06	18.9%▼	0.86
WB*	3.74	65.5%▼	1.29	172.9%▲	3.52
Total	3.82	16.0%▼	3.21	37.4%▲	4.41

*The UPN and WB networks shut down in 2006 and quickly merged to form the still-operational CW network.

TAKEN FROM: Parents Television Council, *Dying to Entertain: Violence on Prime Time Broadcast Television 1998–2006*, January 10, 2007.

is often substantially sanitized, with little focus on the victim, his or her injuries or pain, or other long-term consequences. Finally, television depictions glamorize and justify the use of violence as an appropriate response, with perpetrators rarely displaying remorse or being criticized. In many cases, it is the "good guy" who engages in violence. Overall, the context in which violence is presented on television serves to trivialize its impact and legitimize its use.

TV Characters Model Behavior

Along with parents, peers, schools, and other institutions, television represents an important socializing influence on children's propensity to engage in violence. Television characters model how to perpetrate violence and are often rewarded for their actions. When these models are perceived as attractive and their behaviors as justified, young people are more likely to imitate their actions. Television portrayals also provide scripts about various scenarios and what responses are appropriate. When uncertain about how to behave in a situation, youth may utilize such scripts to guide their behavior. Additionally, high exposure to television may cultivate a perceived social reality among viewers that is largely rooted in media representations. If such perceptions are based on violent programming, young people are likely to see themselves as living in a dangerous world where aggressive behaviors have considerable value.

After decades of research and more than a thousand studies, the answer is yes, watching violent content on television affects youth. Although not all those exposed will commit violent acts, the evidence is overwhelming that viewing high levels of violent programming increases the likelihood of aggression. As with other learned behaviors, many factors at the individual, family, and broader community levels contribute to the development of aggression; however, media violence is clearly a risk factor. In fact, findings from research that combines the results of hundreds of individual studies suggest that about 10 percent of real-life violence may be attributed to media violence.

| *"Those who propose that media violence causes aggression have greatly over-stated the results of the research."*

Television Violence Does Not Contribute to Aggressive Behavior in Young People

Jonathan Freedman

Jonathan Freedman is a professor of psychology at the University of Toronto and the author of Media Violence and Its Effect on Aggression: Assessing the Scientific Evidence. *In the following viewpoint, Freedman repudiates the 2007 findings of the Federal Communications Commission (FCC) that called for restricting violent television programming to late evening hours because of the presumed relationship between violent imagery and increases in aggression among young viewers. Freedman claims the sup-posed connection between fictional violence and real-world ag-gression are not based on scientific evidence; instead, he asserts that the FCC's recommendation stems from conjecture. Freed-man contends that the statistical evidence showing decreases in youth violence clearly indicates that fictional depictions of vio-lence are not translating into real-world crimes.*

As you read, consider the following questions:

1. Why does Freedman believe the FCC misunderstood the findings of the 2001 surgeon general's report on television violence?

2. About how many research reports on the effects of television violence on viewers have been published, according to the author?

3. Since what year have violent crime statistics leveled off and begun to decline, as Freedman reports?

It is unfortunate that the Federal Communications Commission [FCC] has recently [in April 2007] concluded that exposure to media violence increases aggression. Despite what the report says, the scientific evidence does not support the hypothesis that exposure to media violence causes people to be aggressive. This was true in 1984 when I published my first review of this literature; it was true in 2002 when I published my comprehensive review of the research; and it is true now. Those who propose that media violence causes aggression have greatly overstated the results of the research, and have generally ignored findings that contradict their views.

No Scientific Evidence to Back FCC Claims

Moreover, as weak as the evidence is for an effect on aggression, it is virtually nonexistent for an effect on real violence. The FCC cites the surgeon general's 2001 report on youth violence to support the view that exposure to television violence causes aggression (in the short run). However, the FCC does not seem to accept the surgeon general's clear conclusion that exposure to media violence is not a risk factor for real violence. This picking and choosing of what to cite is a major weakness in the latest FCC report.

The FCC suggests that the type of violence portrayed and the outcomes of that violence determine how strong the effect is on aggression. I repeat, the research does not indicate any effect on aggression regardless of the type of violence. It is also important to note that there is no evidence that one kind of portrayal of violence, including whether the violence is punished or not, rewarded or not, legitimate or not, has more effect on aggression than another. That there are such differences is mere speculation that the FCC cites as if there were evidence for it. Similarly, there is no consistent evidence that more-aggressive people are affected more than less-aggressive people. Any assertions about this are based on some people's intuitions but not on scientific research.

The FCC report often seems to equate those who know something about the research with those who do not. For example, the report says that there has been "some dispute regarding the amount of research" on the effect of television violence. It notes that the American Academy of Pediatrics [AAP] refers to more than 3,500 studies, whereas [psychologist Edward] Donnerstein says there are about 250. This is not a dispute between those with equal knowledge. Everyone who knows anything about the field agrees that there are fewer than 300 studies. That the AAP says there are 3,500-plus studies simply indicates how out of touch that group is with the research.

Conjecture Instead of Research

In much of the report, including the examples just cited, the FCC does not make a sufficient distinction between people's opinions, intuitions and musings on the one hand, and the hard scientific data on the other. This is really a shame. The FCC had the opportunity to conduct a serious, in-depth review of the research on the effect of media violence. It could have read all of the research, assessed the methodology, looked for strengths and weaknesses in every study, and evaluated the results. If the readers had been trained scientists and approached the task with open minds, this report would have

The Nanny Government

Parents have the tools they need to protect their children. If the government steps in and regulates the content of television shows or relegates certain shows to a late-night or early-morning hour, it steps over the line and becomes the Federal Babysitting Agency—replacing parents as the ultimate decisionmakers.

The power to control the upbringing of children, including what they watch, should remain in the most capable, effective, and constitutional hands possible: the parents.

Caroline Fredrickson,
Christian Science Monitor, *September 6, 2007.*

been very valuable and could have provided the basis for conclusions rooted in science. Sadly, this apparently was not done.

Regrettably, the FCC commissioners seem to have relied mainly on what various experts told them about the research, and did not clearly distinguish between those who based their opinions on solid research and those who did not. Although the personal opinions of experts can be helpful, they cannot provide the scientific basis for a review.

Ultimately, it is the *findings* that matter—not what people think about them or tell you about them. That I happen to believe the research does not show a causal effect of media violence while others think it does is interesting, but of little or no scientific value. We do not reach scientific conclusions by consensus, but by looking at what the research shows.

It is likewise important to keep in mind that virtually all of the research and all of my statements above refer to fictional or fictionalized depictions of violence, not to images of real violence in the news or in sports. There is too little evidence to know anything about the effect of media coverage of real violence. However, I would argue that anyone who believes that exposure to fictional violence has harmful effects should surely accept that exposure to real violence must have at least the same kind of effects and probably stronger ones.

Rates of Violent Crime Are Decreasing

One of the glaring omissions in the report is the lack of discussion of one of the strongest arguments against the idea that media violence causes aggression. The rate of violent crime in the United States increased sharply from 1965 to 1980, and some people blamed that increase on television. The rate of violent crime leveled off until about 1992. Since that time, television continued to have violent programs, and many films contained vivid scenes of extreme violence. There was also more rap music with violent words, and, of course, video games with violent themes became extremely popular, especially among young males.

If exposure to violent media causes aggression and violent behavior, one would surely expect the rate of violent crime to have gone through the roof. Yet, since 1992 there has been a dramatic drop in violent crime, including violent crime committed by young males, to the point that it is now below what it was when television was introduced many decades ago. It seems obvious that media violence did not cause the earlier increase just as it did not cause the more recent decrease. Proponents of the notion that media violence is harmful hate to hear this mentioned and have no serious response to it. They would rather not discuss it.

To summarize: The FCC report is not based on a thorough, objective review of the scientific research. It has reached conclusions that may be politically expedient but are not justified by the scientific research. The fact is simple: there is no convincing evidence that exposure to any form of media violence causes people to become more aggressive and none at all that it causes them to commit violent crimes.

Periodical Bibliography

The following articles have been selected to supplement the diverse views presented in this chapter.

Bill Blake — "Go Ahead, Steal My Car," *Chronicle of Higher Education*, June 27, 2009.

James Bowman — "Look at Me," *American Spectator*, October 2009.

Economist — "Good Game?" May 30, 2009.

Kevin A. Hassett — "The Games We Play," *National Review*, October 22, 2007.

Stephen Marche — "What's Really Going on with All These Vampires?" *Esquire*, November 2009.

Cheryl K. Olson, Lawrence Kutner, and Eugene V. Beresin — "Children and Video Games: How Much Do We Know?" *Psychiatric Times*, October 2007.

Kathryn Reklis — "Prime-Time Torture," *Christian Century*, June 3, 2008.

Joe Saltzman — "Paparazzi to Go," *USA Today* (magazine), November 2009.

Bret Stephens — "Celebrity Culture vs. the Right Stuff," *Wall Street Journal*, July 21, 2009.

Benjamin Svetkey et al. — "Celebrity in Chief," *Entertainment Weekly*, November 28, 2008.

CHAPTER 4

How Is U.S. Popular Culture Received Around the World?

Chapter Preface

During World War II, the entertainment industry—especially Hollywood—took part in the Allied war effort by producing movies that showcased American values of honor and righteousness while presenting America as a melting pot of ethnic diversity. Movies such as *Flying Tigers* (1942), *Air Force* (1943), and *Bataan* (1943) also emphasized U.S. commitment to its besieged allies in China and the Philippines, and they demonstrated America's determination not to surrender friendly ground to foreign invaders. The U.S. State Department even commissioned Walt Disney to tour Latin America and South America in the early 1940s to create animated features that would show goodwill between America and its neighbors to the south. Although all of these celluloid efforts were purely propagandistic and meant to strengthen America's resolve and maintain friendly relations with as many nations as possible during wartime, they did present a very positive image of American values, including the duty to help foreign countries fight a just war.

Martha Bayles, a humanities and literature professor and author of *Hole in Our Soul: The Loss of Beauty and Meaning in American Popular Music*, believes that the boostering America did during the 1940s and even through the subsequent three decades (as the Cold War against communism ran its course) has given way since the 1980s to an unattractive media glut that shows no concern for how the nation's image is presented worldwide. Bayles insists that American pop culture exports—film, music, and television—are saturated with violence, nudity, profanity, and a general crass commercialism that sends a very negative message to foreign markets. Noting that U.S. citizens are concerned about these messages at home, she wonders how they are received in parts of the world that have more conservative cultural morals. In addition, Bayles worries that the continual growth of these industries and the numerous products they dispense has not been slowed by a popular backlash that could perhaps compel the media to take notice of the damage being done. "Instead of questioning whether Americans should be super-sizing to others the same cultural diet that is giving us indigestion at home, we still seem to congratulate ourselves that our popular culture now pervades just about every society on Earth, including many that would rather keep it out," Bayles writes. She insists that "American popular culture is no longer a beacon of freedom" and is conversely projecting images of a violent, warlike society that breeds intolerance and imperialism. In a post-9/11 world, she argues that America must show that "freedom is self-correcting—that Americans have not only liberty but also a civilization worthy of liberty."

In the following viewpoints, several cultural critics debate how American pop culture is perceived overseas. Some agree with Bayles that the music, film, and television industries are projecting negative images that feed foreign fears of the pervasive influence of coarse American values. Others contend that America's cultural exports are merely melding with those from other nations, creating a global culture that all people can share. Regardless of whose argument seems more persuasive, critics of various stripes recognize—as Bayles writes—that American pop culture is "our de facto ambassador to the world" and undoubtedly shapes the way in which the rest of the world views America.

> *"Reactions to American culture—popular culture—profoundly shape the world's attitudes toward the United States."*

U.S. Pop Culture Exports Are Tarnishing the Country's Global Image

Robert Royal

American popular culture is often portrayed as the single most influential culture worldwide. American music, movies, television programs, and video games are exported globally and consumed by individuals on every continent. Still, many people, both in America and abroad, lament the proliferation of a culture they see as profane and violent. In the following viewpoint, Robert Royal argues that American popular culture is providing the rest of the world with a skewed version of American life and beliefs. He contends that many outsiders only see the sensationalist cultural exports and do not understand that Americans as a whole do not value the ideals transmitted in these works. As a result, Royal suggests that American pop culture be reformed and

Robert Royal, "America, the Pop Culture Superpower: Our Popular Culture Distorts Who We Really Are and Fuels Hostility," *National Catholic Reporter*, vol. 42, September 29, 2006, p. 21. Copyright © The National Catholic Reporter Publishing Company. Reprinted by permission of *National Catholic Reporter*, 115 E. Armour Blvd., Kansas City, MO 64111. www.ncronline.org.

repackaged before its current negative connotations ruin America's global image permanently. Robert Royal is the president of the Faith and Reason Institute, a think-tank located in Washington, D.C., and dedicated to the promotion of faith and reason as central modes of understanding the human experience.

As you read, consider the following questions:

1. According to the author, what was the significance of popular culture during the Enlightenment?

2. What are the two principal problems with American popular culture, as stated by Royal?

3. What are the four principles that the author suggests should guide Americans in the struggle to redefine the negative international view of America?

My wife and I drove up Mount Zion toward Jerusalem a few years ago and got stuck in traffic. I was somewhat drunk on the Old Testament phrase repeating in my head, "I shall go up to Jerusalem." My wife turned on the radio, and what I can only call Hebrew rap music came on. We agreed that America was going to have a lot to answer for someday.

That day has, of course, long since come. We Westerners once thought modern communications were bringing the world closer together. Those hopes were partly correct, mostly among peoples who already shared a good deal. Yet they have also proved illusory. Some cultures encounter alien ways and are repelled. Others may envy and imitate. Still others may be threatened.

The United States is the sole remaining superpower in this realm too. In the postmodern international order, all three of these reactions to American culture—popular culture—profoundly shape the world's attitudes toward the United States.

American Pop Culture's Negative Message

Popular culture took on social importance in the reaction against an earlier form of globalization: the universal civilization promised by the Enlightenment. Among 19th-century German Romantics, the mores, folk stories, songs and beliefs of the people were values tied to a particular tribe or nation and resistant to France's claim to a universal civilization. Though Enlightenment universalism has self-destructed, we all still feel a tension between our desire for modern benefits that stem from global civilization and our natural attachments to beliefs and practices we regard as sacred and threatened.

An American, especially a Christian, will sympathize. We're sorry that we have the decadent popular culture we do at home, and we're even sorrier to be exporting it. There are two principal problems with American popular culture. First, American popular culture is corrupt and corrupting. There is no need to repeat the familiar litany of sex, drugs and violence. But these all-too-human elements also appear in the Old Testament. Our genius has been to glorify and glamorize bad behavior in music, films and television. Many other cultures, some decadent and some not, resent it bitterly.

The second problem involves what our exported culture leaves out. Any American who follows the trail will be shocked at how much never makes it through the pop culture filters. If you tell a group of foreigners, for example, that 90 percent of Americans are believers who practice religion, you will get wide stares: What about [pop icons and sex symbols] Britney [Spears] and Madonna, [shock rocker] Marilyn Manson and [photographer Robert] Mapplethorpe? Or you will get misinterpretation: We know your media and ours claim that your government is conspiring to impose a theocracy on America, convert Muslims in the Middle East, and bring about Armageddon in Israel.

At others times, this schizophrenia (America is bad, libertine or Puritanical) would not matter. In the current context

Foreign Youth on America

One of the few efforts to measure the impact of popular culture abroad was made by Louisiana State University researchers Melvin and Margaret DeFleur, who in 2003 polled teenagers in 12 countries: Saudi Arabia, Bahrain, South Korea, Mexico, China, Spain, Taiwan, Lebanon, Pakistan, Nigeria, Italy and Argentina. Their conclusion, while tentative, is nonetheless suggestive: "The depiction of Americans in media content as violent, of American women as sexually immoral and of many Americans engaging in criminal acts has brought many of these 1,313 youthful subjects to hold generally negative attitudes toward people who live in the United States."

Martha Bayles, Washington Post, *August 28, 2005.*

of Islamic fundamentalism, it only adds fuel to several fires. But let us not deceive ourselves. Even without our obvious faults and the fantastic claims, many people hate us. Sayyid Qutb, a founder of Egypt's Muslim Brotherhood, was pro-American until he visited the United States from 1948 to 1951. He left disgusted because in those innocent pre-Elvis years he saw men and women dancing together at church-sponsored social events. Many since have adopted the same view on much more substantial grounds.

Rehabilitating the U.S. Image Abroad

What do we do about this part of the international struggle? There are benefits and drawbacks to every approach, but four principles might guide us:

- We need to distinguish between anger over cultural imperialism and envy of the power of our "relatively undeveloped culture," a phrase much used in France. America has much to offer the world and the world has imitated our virtues, as well as our vices.

- We need to clean house for its own sake, knowing no amount of reform will satisfy everyone abroad. American men and women will dance together publicly in any foreseeable future and, by and large, we should be happy they do.

- American pluralism, civil rights, religious toleration, and equality before the law are values that we proudly defend—with arguments and information first, with more substantial means when necessary. Both the U.S. government and private institutions have largely abandoned the kind of public information services we used to provide even in friendly countries in the form of libraries of American books and periodicals, cultural events and lectures. We need more of this again.

- American culture is not a universal civilization but neither is it the depths of depravity. America is conspicuously open within certain notions of liberty. We grew great because we absorbed many things from many quarters. We would grow smaller if we stopped that process. But our political, cultural, and religious institutions need to do a much better job in portraying what is good with us, even as we wrestle over fixing what's bad.

The truth sets us free. Telling real if surprising truths about America while we try to heal our culture is essential if we hope for better lives at home and with the rest of the world.

> "*The continuing and indeed growing relevance of local economic connections suggests that cultural imperialism will not prove to be the dominant trend.*"

Some Countries Remain Resistant to U.S. Pop Culture Exports

Tyler Cowen

In the following viewpoint, economics professor Tyler Cowen makes the case that many local cultures are refusing to assimilate American popular culture into their existing culture. Cowen contends that many emerging economic powers, such as India and China, with a strong sense of identity are holding strongly to their national culture and actively producing and consuming their own pop culture while increasingly rejecting exports from the United States. Thus, he makes the claim that Western cultural dominance is unlikely. Tyler Cowen teaches economics at George Mason University and is coauthor of the blog Marginal Revolution.

As you read, consider the following questions:

1. What percentage of the Indian music market is produced domestically, according to Cowen?

2. The author believes that American popular culture is most popular under what circumstances?

3. As stated by Cowen, international moviegoers are beginning to look for non-Hollywood films from what other sources?

American movies and music have done very well in some countries like Sweden and less well in others like India. This may sound like a simple difference in human tastes, but decisions to consume culture have an economic aspect.

Loyalties to cultural goods and services—be it heavy metal music or the opera—are about social networking and choosing an identity and an aspiration. That is, we use culture to connect with other people and to define ourselves; both are, to some extent, economic decisions. The continuing and indeed growing relevance of local economic connections suggests that cultural imperialism will not prove to be the dominant trend.

Defining Oneself Through Local Culture

Local culture commands loyalty when people are involved in networks of status and caste, and they pursue religious and communal markers of identity. Those individuals use local cultural products to signal their place in hierarchies.

An Indian Muslim might listen to religious Qawwali music to set himself apart from local Hindus, or a native of Calcutta might favor songs from Bengali [an Indian language] cinema. The Indian music market is 96 percent domestic in origin, in part because India is such a large and multifaceted society. Omar Lizardo, an assistant professor of sociology at the University of Notre Dame, explains this logic in his recent paper "Globalization and Culture: A Sociological Perspective."

Today, economic growth is booming in countries where American popular culture does not dominate, namely India and China. Population growth is strong in many Islamic countries, which typically prefer local music and get their news from sources like the satellite broadcaster Al Jazeera [an Arabic-language news network].

The combination of these trends means that American entertainment, for largely economic reasons, will lose relative standing in the global marketplace. In fact, Western culture often creates its own rivals by bringing creative technologies like the recording studio or the printing press to foreign lands.

Markers of Global Identity

American popular culture tends to be popular when people interact with others from around the world and seek markers of global identity. My stepdaughter spent last summer studying French in Nice, with students from many other countries. They ate and hung out at McDonald's, a name and symbol they all share, even though it was not everyone's favorite meal.

Globalization is most likely to damage local culture in regions like Scandinavia that are lightly populated, not very hierarchical and looking for new global cultural symbols. But the rest of the world's population is in countries—China and India, of course, but also Brazil, Mexico, Egypt and Indonesia—that do not fit that description.

"American" cultural products rely increasingly on non-American talent and international symbols and settings. [The movie] *Babel*, which won this year's [2007] Golden Globe for best drama, has a Mexican director, and is set in Morocco, Japan and Mexico, mostly with non-English dialogue.

Hollywood movies are popular in Europe in part because of the successes of European welfare states and of European economic integration. Western Europe has become more equal in its treatment of citizens, it has moved away from an aristocratic class society, and it has strong global connections. All

U.S. Cultural Imperialism's Downside

Cultural imperialism involves much more than simple consumer goods; it involves the dissemination of ostensibly American principles, such as freedom and democracy. Though this process might sound appealing on the surface, it masks a frightening truth: many cultures around the world are gradually disappearing due to the overwhelming influence of corporate and cultural America.

The motivations behind American cultural imperialism parallel the justifications for U.S. imperialism throughout history: the desire for access to foreign markets and the belief in the superiority of American culture. . . . According to the [British newspaper the] *Guardian*, American films accounted for approximately 80 percent of global box office revenue in January 2003. And who can forget good old Micky D's? With over 30,000 restaurants in over one hundred countries, the ubiquitous golden arches of McDonald's are now, according to [American journalist] Eric Schlosser's *Fast Food Nation*, "more widely recognized than the Christian cross." Such American domination inevitably hurts local markets, as the majority of foreign industries are unable to compete with the economic strength of U.S. industry. Because it serves American economic interests, corporations conveniently ignore the detrimental impact of American control of foreign markets.

Julia Galeota,
Humanist, *May–June 2004.*

those factors favor an interest in American and global popular culture; Hollywood movies often capture 70 percent or more of a typical European cinematic market. Social democracy, which the Europeans often hold up in opposition to the American model, in fact aided this cultural invasion by making Europe more egalitarian.

The End of American Cultural Dominance

Many smaller countries have been less welcoming of cultural imports. It is common in Central America for domestically produced music to command up to 70 percent of market share. In Ghana, domestic music has captured 71 percent of the market, according to Unesco [United Nations Educational Scientific and Cultural Organization] figures. Critics of cultural imperialism charge that rich cultures dominate poor ones. But the data supplied by Professor Lizardo show that the poorer a country, the more likely it will buy and listen to its own domestic music. This makes sense given that music is a form of social networking and the relevant networks are primarily local.

That said, the poorest countries don't produce many of the films they watch. Making a movie costs much more than cutting an album. So as the world becomes richer, the relative market share of Hollywood movies will probably fall more than the relative market share of American popular music. Furthermore, moviegoers are starting to look to Bollywood [Indian-made] films, or other Asian productions, rather than Hollywood, for their markers of global identity.

The complaint of "cultural imperialism" is looking increasingly implausible. As I argued in *Creative Destruction: How Globalization Is Changing the World's Cultures*, the funk of [American musician] James Brown helped shape the music of West Africa; Indian authors draw upon [British author] Charles Dickens; and Arabic pop is centered in France and Belgium. Western cultural exports are as likely to refresh foreign art forms as to destroy them. Western technologies—from the metal carving knife to acrylic paint to digital filmmaking—have spurred creativity worldwide.

Culture is not a zero-sum game, so the greater reach of one culture does not necessarily mean diminished stature for others. In the broad sweep of history, many different traditions have grown together and flourished. American popular culture will continue to make money, but the 21st century will bring a broad mélange of influences, with no clear world cultural leader.

> "The same Europeans who heap con-
> tempt on American politics, cuisine and
> fashion apparently can't seem to get
> enough of our arsenal of expletives."

Europeans Are Adopting American Pop Culture's Use of Profanity

Elizabeth Lev

In the following viewpoint, Elizabeth Lev takes issue with the global proliferation of American profanity. Lev argues that curse words have become one of the main cultural artifacts exported through American popular culture. The author asserts that even though this language is not typical of everyday speech in the United States, individuals outside of the country have come to view it as characteristic of the way Americans communicate. Lev laments the passing of previous American popular culture works and icons whose utterance of such base language would have been unthinkable. Elizabeth Lev is an American art historian who lives and works in Rome.

Elizabeth Lev, "Exporting Expletives: America's Contribution to Global Culture," *Politics Daily*, November 20, 2009. Content © 2010 AOL Inc. Used with permission.

As you read, consider the following questions:

1. What are some of the English profanities that Lev observes Europeans uttering?

2. As stated by the author, popular culture has suggested that a "fluency in profanity" is tied to what?

3. According to Lev, what does the use of profanity underscore, and how do these words function in speech?

It started like a scene from an E.M. Forster novel [by the British author exploring class differences in the early twentieth century]. In a quiet Tuscan retreat, a handsome, well-dressed young man played piano in an exquisitely arranged drawing room. What he lacked in artistry, he made up for with gusto, and soon enough a weary British father asked him to curtail his musical efforts for the evening as there was a small child sleeping upstairs. The young man rose, shrugged his elegant shoulders and drawled in lightly Spanish-flavored English, "I don't f**king see why I f**king should, I f**king paid for this place same as you f**king did."

Saucer-eyed, the father pressed his request, but was met with further torrents of profanity until he retreated into the manager's office.

A few days later, in a coffee shop three blocks from St. Peter's, a Roman gentleman was attempting to impress a young woman with his linguistic ability and political savoir-faire. "These politicians are all full of s**t." he proclaimed airily, waving manicured hands, "I say f**k them all."

A group of fresh faced Roman school kids, perched outside the venerable remains of the Coliseum, eagerly flaunted their English to a group of elderly American tourists, calling out cheerily: "What's your name?" "Where are you from?" "F**k you!"

The same Europeans who heap contempt on American politics, cuisine and fashion apparently can't seem to get enough of our arsenal of expletives.

Rise of Profanity in American Pop Culture

The ease with which English profanity currently falls from the lips of non-English-speaking Europeans indicates that many denizens of the Old World think that is how we speak in the wilds of the New. The Greeks once coined the term "barbarian" to mimic the babbling sound of strangers' language; today it is the Anglophones [English speakers] who appear as barely civilized grunters.

Where would they get the idea that Americans routinely punctuate their speech with foul language? After all, one rarely hears profanity in an American diner or department store, nor does it appear in our newspapers. Perhaps part of the cause can be found in the tinny pop music that echoes from every iPod and the repartee issuing from the lips of our golden, glamorous film stars. Among "artists," profanity has become as cool in the 21st century as smoking was in the days of [Hollywood film stars] Bogey [Humphrey Bogart], [Lauren] Bacall and [jazz singer] Billie Holiday.

In 1939, [film character] Rhett Butler shocked cinemagoers by tamely declaring, "Frankly, my dear, I don't give a damn." One can only imagine what *Gone with the Wind* viewers would have made of five minutes of [film director] Quentin Tarantino dialogue?

It strains the imagination to picture [mid-twentieth century actresses] Grace Kelly or Audrey Hepburn in their exquisite costumes and coiffures contorting their polished features and spewing out curses. Yet Charlize Theron and Angelina Jolie string a few "ands" and "thes" among four letter words, and, voila, Oscar! Power and conviction in a performance seem strangely proportionate to the use of profanity.

Paris Hilton Mirrors America

Despite her fame and good fortune, for most sentient adults [hotel heiress Paris] Hilton personifies the decadence of our cultural moment. With her nightclub brawls, her endless sexcapades, her vapid interviews, her rodent-like dog, and her lack of ostensible talent, she reeks of every vice ever ascribed to our poor country. She has become a synonym for American materialism, bad manners, greed, "like" and "whatever" Valley Girl inarticulateness, parochialism [narrow-mindedness], arrogance, promiscuity, antifeminism, exposed roots and navels, entitlement, cell-phone addiction, anorexia and bulimia, predilection for gas-guzzling private transportation, pornified womanhood, exhibitionism, narcissism—you name it.

Paris deserves almost all of this. You don't need to share [Islamic terrorist leader] Osama bin Laden's view of America to see that Paris mirrors us at our contemporary worst. But something still doesn't compute: Why, if Paris says so much about us, do Americans—not just college professors and the commentariat but celebrity watchers and tabloid junkies—hate her so much? And why, if she is so offensive, is she so ubiquitous?

Kay S. Hymowitz,
City Journal, *Autumn 2006.*

The Cross-Cultural Exchange of Profanity

Our legions of college-age students studying abroad in Europe with its lax drinking laws have fostered this new Anglo-invasion, as has our anonymous Internet chatter, which frequently takes coarse language as a new form of philosophical exposition.

It seems sad that a language that saw creative invectives brought to a high art (think of Shakespeare's "paunchy onion-eyed lout") has sunk so low. Even [*Moby Dick* author] Herman Melville's rough whalers sailing alone in untamed waters never manage more than a "poor pegging lubber." Now [American comedian] George Carlin's "seven words you can't say on television" seem to be the staple of song lyrics and the ceiling of cinematic artistic expression.

Some claim that the F-word has been rendered innocuous by common usage particularly in music and cinema. How many movies have featured an angelic child parting rosebud lips to emit the F-bomb to the delight and amazement of elders? How many parents and children sing along to a catchy tune, awkwardly humming through the expletives they wouldn't use themselves? Pop culture suggests fluency in profanity has become the modern rite of passage into adulthood.

An Unrepresentative Sample of Language

Despite these attempts to render profanity palatable, they serve only to underscore our inability to communicate. Expletives fill empty places in speech, when one is at a loss of something to say. In the absence of serious argumentative force, a well-placed profanity seems to fill the logic gap. Abusive expletives can deflect others' attacks or bolster a flailing rebuttal the way [former British prime minister] Winston Churchill would raise his voice when he thought his points were particularly weak. Far from a contemporary display of sophistication, it is a retreat from engagement, looking to nonplus the interlocutor without ever engaging the argument.

The fact is most American's don't speak this way. We remain a people of polite phrasing; "have a nice day" and "I beg your pardon," are more common to our everyday speech than profanity. The average American would have as much difficulty sparring in the expletive arena as he would in a street fight.

Consequently those of more refined speech find themselves drowned out by the cussing brigade, who often have less to say but garner much attention saying it.

The poster child for the new Anglophone approach of substituting invective for argument is singer Lily Allen, who recently released a little ditty slamming those who oppose gay marriage. In her defense of love of all sorts, she warbles in her childlike voice, "F**k you, f**k you very very much, 'cause we hate what you do and we hate your whole crew, so please don't stay in touch."

As Allen's song plays unedited in my Roman coffee shop, and waiters, children and little old ladies chime in with the catchy words of the refrain, one wonders how the language that gave the world the lyrics of [American musical writer and director] Oscar Hammerstein, the witty repartee of [American movie stars] Katharine Hepburn and Jimmy Stewart, and the sparkling polemics of [American authors] Mary McCarthy and William F. Buckley has been reduced to exporting profanity, the abandonment of intellect for insult.

> "There is a sense overseas today that America's cultural exports are not as important, or as alluring, as they once were."

American Cultural Exports Are Losing Their Global Dominance

Richard Pells

Many people in America and around the world argue that American pop culture has dominated the global marketplace, quashing indigenous arts and leading to a global monoculture. Richard Pells, however, argues in the viewpoint that follows that American culture has recently lost its appeal and supremacy as a result of globalization. Pells acknowledges that throughout the twentieth century, all those who encountered American culture eagerly consumed it, but he maintains that such enthusiastic consumption of all things American has virtually ceased in the first decade of the twenty-first century. Pells also attributes the shift in global opinion to the increase in number of international student exchange programs and the prominence of the Internet as a means of disseminating knowledge. Richard Pells is an

Richard Pells, "Does the World Still Care About American Culture?" *Chronicle of Higher Education*, vol. 55, March 6, 2009, pp. B4–B5. Copyright © 2009 by The Chronicle of Higher Education. Reproduced by permission of the author.

American history professor at the University of Texas, Austin and the author of the books Not Like Us: How Europeans Have Loved, Hated, and Transformed American Culture Since World War II *and* Modernist America: Art, Music, Movies, and the Global Impact of American Culture.

As you read, consider the following questions:

1. What artists during what time period were most successful in terms of international appeal, according to Pells?

2. As stated by the author, what percentage of ticket sales in France did American movies account for in 1998 and 2008?

3. What two devices does Pells claim have made it possible for individuals to access whatever culture and information they choose at any time?

For most of the 20th century, the dominant culture in the world was American. Now that is no longer true. What is most striking about attitudes toward the United States in other countries is not the anti-Americanism they reflect, or the disdain for former President George W. Bush, or the opposition to American foreign policies. Rather, people abroad are increasingly indifferent to America's culture.

American culture used to be the elephant in everyone's living room. Whether people felt uncomfortable with the omnipresence of America's high or popular culture in their countries, they could not ignore its power or its appeal. American writers and artists were superstars—the objects of curiosity, admiration, and envy. Today they are for the most part unnoticed, or regarded as ordinary mortals, participants in a global rather than a distinctively American culture.

America's elections still matter to people overseas. As someone who has taught American studies in Europe, Latin

America, and Asia, I received e-mail messages from friends abroad asking me who I thought would win the presidency in November [2008]. But I rarely get queries about what I think of the latest American movie. Nor does anyone ask me about American novelists, playwrights, composers, or painters.

A Bygone Era

Imagine any of these events or episodes in the past happening now: In 1928, fresh from having written "Rhapsody in Blue" and the "Piano Concerto in F Major," George Gershwin traveled to Paris and Vienna. He was treated like an idol. As America's most famous composer, he met with many of the leading European modernists: [composers Arnold] Schoenberg, [Igor] Stravinsky, [Serge] Prokofiev, [Maurice] Ravel. At one point, Gershwin asked Stravinsky if he could take lessons from the great Russian. Stravinsky responded by asking Gershwin how much money he made in a year. Told the answer was in six figures, Stravinsky quipped, "In that case, . . . I should study with you."

In the 1930s, [American jazz musicians] Louis Armstrong and Duke Ellington toured throughout Europe, giving concerts to thousands of adoring fans, including members of the British royal family. In the 1940s and 50s, [American jazz musicians] Dave Brubeck, Miles Davis, Dizzy Gillespie, Benny Goodman, and Charlie Parker often gave concerts in Western and Eastern Europe, the Soviet Union, the Middle East, Africa, Asia, and Latin America. The Voice of America's [America's international public broadcasting system's] most popular program in the 1960s was a show called Music USA, specializing in jazz, with an estimated 100 million listeners around the world. In the 1940s and 50s as well, [American conductor and composer] Leonard Bernstein was invited to conduct symphony orchestras in London, Moscow, Paris, Prague, Tel Aviv, and the La Scala opera house in Milan.

If you were a professor of modern literature at a foreign university, your reading list had to include [American authors Saul] Bellow, [John] Dos Passos, [William] Faulkner, [Ernest] Hemingway, and [John] Steinbeck. If you taught courses on the theater, it was obligatory to discuss [the American plays] *Death of a Salesman, The Iceman Cometh, Long Day's Journey Into Night,* and *A Streetcar Named Desire.*

If you wanted to study modern art, you did not—like [American actor] Gene Kelly in [the movie] *An American in Paris*—journey to the City of Light [Paris] (all the while singing and dancing to the music of Gershwin) to learn how to become a painter. Instead you came to New York, to sit at the feet of [American painters] Willem de Kooning and Jackson Pollock. Or later you hung out at [American pop artist] Andy Warhol's "factory," surrounded by celebrities from the arts and the entertainment world.

If dance was your specialty, where else could you find more creative choreographers than Bob Fosse or Jerome Robbins? If you were an aspiring filmmaker in the 1970s, the movies worth seeing and studying all originated in America. What other country could boast of such cinematic talent as [directors] Woody Allen, Robert Altman, Francis Ford Coppola, George Lucas, Martin Scorsese, and Steven Spielberg?

A Declining Interest

Of course, there are still American cultural icons who mesmerize a global audience or whose photos are pervasive in the pages of the world's tabloid newspapers. [American rock musician] Bruce Springsteen can always pack an arena wherever he performs. The Broadway musical *Rent* has been translated into more than 20 languages. Hollywood's blockbusters still make millions of dollars abroad. America's movie stars remain major celebrities at international film festivals.

But there is a sense overseas today that America's cultural exports are not as important, or as alluring, as they once were.

When I lecture abroad on contemporary American culture, I find that few of America's current artists and intellectuals are household names, luminaries from whom foreigners feel they need to learn. The cultural action is elsewhere—not so much in Manhattan or San Francisco but in Berlin (the site of a major film festival) and Mumbai (the home of Indian filmmakers and media entrepreneurs who are now investing in the movies of Spielberg and other American directors). The importance of Mumbai was reinforced, spectacularly, when *Slumdog Millionaire* won the [2009] Oscar for best picture.

What accounts for the decline of interest in American art, literature, and music? Why has American culture become just another item on the shelves of the global supermarket?

Globalization Dims U.S. Influence

The main answer is that globalization has subverted America's influence. During the 1990s, many people assumed that the emergence of what they called a global culture was just another mechanism for the "Americanization" of the world. Be it Microsoft or McDonald's, Disney theme parks or shopping malls, the movies or the Internet, the artifacts of American culture seemed ubiquitous and inescapable.

Yet far from reinforcing the impact of American culture, globalization has strengthened the cultures of other nations, regions, and continents. Instead of defining what foreigners want, America's cultural producers find themselves competing with their counterparts abroad in shaping people's values and tastes. What we have in the 21st century is not a hegemonic American culture but multiple forms of art and entertainment—voices, images, and ideas that can spring up anywhere and be disseminated all over the planet.

American television programs like [prime time soap operas from the 80's] *Dallas* and *Dynasty* were once the most popular shows on the airwaves, from Norway to New Zealand. Now many people prefer programs that are locally produced.

European Films Capture More of the European Movie Market

Region	2004	2005	2006	2007	2008 est
European films total	24.6%	24.6%	27.9%	28.6%	28.4%
EUR inc/US co-productions	5.8%	12.5%	5.5%	6.3%	6.8%
US	67.3%	60.2%	63.4%	63.2%	63.2%
Others	2.3%	2.7%	3.2%	1.8%	1.6%
European films by country of origin					
FR France	8.6%	9.2%	10.6%	8.4%	12.6%
GB United Kingdom	4.5%	3.9%	2.8%	6.1%	2.2%
IT Italy	2.2%	2.9%	3.0%	3.8%	3.6%
DE Germany	4.3%	3.2%	4.8%	3.8%	3.5%
ES Spain	2.4%	2.3%	2.8%	2.1%	1.4%
Other EUR Other European countries	2.7%	3.1%	3.9%	4.6%	5.0%

Note: Percentages were calculated based on the number of admissions to films.

TAKEN FROM: European Audiovisual Observatory-LUMIERE database.

Meanwhile cable and satellite facilities permit stations like [Arabic news source] Al-Jazeera to define and interpret the news from a Middle Eastern perspective for people throughout the world.

Since 2000, moreover, American movies have steadily lost market share in Europe and Asia. In 1998, the year in which *Titanic* was released abroad, American films commanded 64 percent of the ticket sales in France. Ten years later, Hollywood's share of the French market has fallen to 50 percent. Similarly, in 1998, American films accounted for 70 percent of the tickets sold in South Korea. Today that figure has fallen to less than 50 percent. As in the case of television programs, audiences increasingly prefer movies made in and about their own countries or regions. Indian films are now more popular in India than are imports from Hollywood. At the same time, American moviegoers are increasingly willing to sample films from abroad (and not just in art houses), which has led to the popularity in the United States of Japanese cartoons and animated films as well as recent German movies like *The Lives of Others*.

Decentralizing Knowledge and Culture

After World War II, professors and students from abroad were eager to study in the United States. America was, after all, the center of the world's intellectual and cultural life. Now, with the rise of continental exchange programs and the difficulties that foreign academics face obtaining U.S. visas, it is often easier for a Dutch student to study in Germany or France, or for a Middle Eastern student to study in India, than for either of them to travel to an American university. That further diminishes the impact of American culture abroad.

Crowds, especially of young people, still flock to McDonald's—whether in Beijing, Moscow, or Paris. But every country has always had its own version of equally popular fast food. There are wurst stands in Germany and Austria, fish-

and-chips shops in England, noodle restaurants in South Korea and Singapore, kabob outlets on street corners in almost any city (including in America), all of which remain popular and compete effectively with the Big Mac.

Finally, cellphones and the Internet make information and culture instantly available to anyone, without having to depend any longer on American definitions of what it is important to know. Indeed, globalization has led not to greater intellectual and political uniformity but to the decentralization of knowledge and culture. We live today in a universe full of cultural options, and we are therefore free to choose what to embrace and what to ignore.

American Culture as One of Many

I am not suggesting that America's culture is irrelevant. It remains one—but only one—of the cultural alternatives available to people abroad and at home. Moreover, it is certainly conceivable that President [Barack] Obama will improve America's currently dreadful image in the world, encouraging people to pay more attention not only to American policies but also to American culture—which the Bush administration, despite its efforts at cultural diplomacy, was never able to do.

But it is doubtful that America will ever again be the world's pre-eminent culture, as it was in the 20th century. That is not a cause for regret. Perhaps we are all better off in a world of cultural pluralism than in a world made in America.

"What people around the world think about American culture may tell us more about these people than about the United States."

International Anti-American Sentiment Has More to Do with American Power than American Culture

Jessica C.E. Gienow-Hecht

The spread of American popular culture is often equated with the rise in anti-American sentiments that have swelled world-wide throughout the twentieth and twenty-first centuries. Some scholars and commentators, however, have questioned whether ascribing such a strong influence to American culture ignores the larger reasons why anti-Americanism exists. In the viewpoint that follows, Jessica C.E. Gienow-Hecht argues that anti-Americanism stems less from the explosion of American popular culture worldwide and more from America's increasing power on the global scene. Further, she maintains that globalization and the increasing cultural exchange by all nations are equally to blame for the disappearance of indigenous cultures, not Ameri-

Jessica C.E. Gienow-Hecht, "A European Considers the Influence of American Culture," *eJournal USA*, February 1, 2006.

can cultural imperialism. Gienow-Hecht concludes that as long as the United States remains a world superpower, anti-American attitudes will continue. Jessica C.E. Gienow-Hecht is a German history professor who has taught both in Germany and the United States. She is the author of two books, Transmission Impossible: American Journalism as Cultural Diplomacy in Postwar Germany, 1945–1955 *and* Sound Diplomacy: Music and Emotions in German-American Relations Since 1850.

As you read, consider the following questions:

1. According to the author, how have Americans historically distinguished themselves from other cultures, and how did they view culture?

2. Based on the 1959 UNESCO study, as cited by Gienow-Hecht, what percentage of the countries surveyed had "official cultural relations programs"?

3. As stated by the author, what is the "fundamental paradox of cultural anti-Americanism"?

In the 1981 film *The Gods Must Be Crazy*, a pilot flying across the Kalahari Desert of Botswana drops an empty Coke bottle into the midst of an African tribe. The natives instantaneously regard the bottle as a gift from their gods. But "the gift" changes the traditions and social mores of their world for the worse. Finally, the natives send a member of the tribe to cast the bottle away over what they believe is the edge of the earth.

This film offers insight into what has come to be known as "The Grand Debate": Are Americans "cultural imperialists" who conquer and corrupt the rest of the world by spreading popular culture everywhere?

It is true, as [American history professor] Richard Pells writes, that much of what constitutes American popular culture today originated in a mélange of foreign influences during the 20th century. But this does not explain why so many people around the world are critical of what they perceive as "American cultural imperialism." Nor does it explain why this idea has become such a force over the past century. If we wish to better understand this perception, we need to consider both the makeup and the influence of American culture abroad—as Pells does—and also its reception by non-Americans.

Culture as Private Entertainment

It is a curious paradox in American history that a nation whose cultural transfers became so controversial started out with little interest in the export of culture. Historically, Americans have found their distinctiveness primarily in their political system rather than in their poets, artists, and novelists. They generally view their popular culture as a source of private entertainment rather than as an instrument of foreign policy. They have never seriously contemplated establishing a department of culture in the federal government. In 1938, the State Department established the Division for Cultural Relations, but many U.S. officials criticized the use of culture as a diplomatic tool. Even today, most Americans believe that culture belongs to the realm of creativity, public taste, and free enterprise, not government.

But following World War II, the situation was different. During the Cold War, American diplomats decided that the United States needed to make the case for the American way of life abroad. At a time when the Soviet Union sought to export communism, public figures as well as policymakers sought to exert more influence through culture around the world. In the years following VE-Day [Victory in Europe Day, ending World War II in Europe], the U.S. government created a number of organizations and programs, such as the United States Information Agency and the Fulbright exchange program, which promoted the transmission of information on American culture.

America Not the First Cultural Exporter

From an objective point of view, of course, the United States was not the first nation to export its way of life. Since the Renaissance, European powers have fostered a variety of cultural exchange programs. The British in India and the Middle East, the Germans in Africa, and the French in Indochina all sent their own culture abroad as a powerful tool to strengthen trade, commerce, and political influence and recruit elites for their own purposes. A 1959 study by UNESCO [United Nations Educational, Scientific, and Cultural Organization] revealed that more than half of the 81 states queried, including all the larger ones, had official cultural relations programs. Some of the European Community's activities today rest on collective cultural diplomacy—that is, the creation of organizations promoting languages and the exchange of cultural information.

Argentina, Mexico, Egypt, Sweden, and India traditionally export their media to adjacent countries. Moreover, the takeover of Hollywood movie studios in recent years by foreign-based corporations has raised the question of whether Americans have changed from "cultural imperialists" to takeover victims. But even if the United States was not the first nation to export its way of life, foreign critics have consistently focused their fears of the future on the United States.

In the 1970s and '80s, for example, Western Europe saw rising anti-American protests, peace groups, and mass demonstrations against the American military presence. In Europe, this anti-Americanism soon expanded to cultural matters. Critics believed that American products exerted an influence that went far beyond their popularity among consumers. U.S. goods seemed to dominate not only foreign markets but foreign minds as well. To many European intellectuals, mass culture, Hollywood movies, and commercialism seemingly threatened European sovereignty, traditions, and a social order based

American Idolatry

Americans of earlier generations . . . listened to music that they admired but could not hope to imitate, because they looked up to a higher plane of culture and technique. Today Americans favor performers with whom they can identify precisely because they have no more technique or culture than the average drunk bellowing into a karaoke machine. Taste descended by degrees. Frank Sinatra sounded more average than Bing Crosby; Elvis Presley more average than Sinatra; The Beatles more average than Elvis; and Bruce Springsteen (or Madonna) about as average as one can get, until *American Idol* came along to elevate what was certified to average.

Spengler, Asia Times, *August 29, 2006.*

on print culture. Mass culture also seemed to blur social distinctions, override nation-state boundaries, and spread the capitalist marketplace.

Yet what Peter tells you about Paul tells you more about Peter than about Paul. What people around the world think about American culture may tell us more about these people than about the United States.

Exaggerated Impact

Today, many politicians and cultural critics around the world lament the influx of U.S. movies. European representatives, for example, are concerned about their cultural distinctiveness and fear that they have already lost much of their audience to American products. Under the headline "The Higher the Satellite, the Lower the Culture," the former French Minister of Culture Jack Lang vehemently condemned U.S. cultural imperialism in a 1991 interview. This criticism was not new. In the 1970s, Chilean professor Armand Mattelart and novelist and critic Ariel Dorfman had written an influential pamphlet titled *Para leer al pato Donald (How To Read Donald Duck)*, which excoriated Hollywood's distorted vision of reality and advocated liberation by the Chilean people of their own culture.

Tiny nations, remote people, and unknown tribes find their way into the headlines of international journals through their vocal protest against Western influences. From Iceland to Latin America, Central Africa to the Philippines, representatives reportedly deplore the demise of their cultures with the rising influence of Anglo-American television and culture.

In many ways, however, the idea of "American cultural imperialism" is inadequate. The American sociologist John Tomlinson has argued that this phenomenon may simply be the spread of modernity, a process of the loss of local cultures and not of cultural expansion. Global technological and economic progress and integration simply lessen the importance of national culture. It is, therefore, misleading to place the blame for a worldwide development on any one nation. Instead, all countries are affected by a global cultural change.

Globalization Changing World Cultures

In the future, the term "globalization" has the potential to replace the criticism of U.S. cultural imperialism. Globalization refers both to the compression of the world and to the growing perception of the earth as an organic whole. Although many speak of globalization as simply an economic phenomenon, it is multidisciplinary in its causes and its effects. The rather vague term includes many characteristics of modernization, such as the spread of Western capitalism, technology, and scientific rationality. The central idea remains, however, that cultures and societies do not necessarily overlap with the boundaries of the nation-state. In other words, the spread of modern mass culture may not be the responsibility of the United States.

In recent decades, much of the international criticism of "cultural imperialism" has moved away from its anti-American line to a more global level, with no one identifiable enemy. Even major critics of the United States have aligned their earlier reproaches along these lines. Already in 1980, Armand Mattelart warned of the broad and inappropriate usage of the notion of "cultural imperialism." He emphasized that the term did not imply an external conspiracy but could only be effected by a combination of international and native (elite) forces.

The Paradox of Anti-Americanism

If the concept of U.S. cultural dominance is so questionable, why then has anti-Americanism ballooned nearly everywhere in the past decades and today? The reasons often have less to do with the United States than with the protesters themselves. In a sense, there is no one cultural anti-Americanism but only a variety of very heterogeneous expressions of this phenomenon, conditioned by geographical concerns and historical cycles. The shape and content of the phenomenon not only differ according to dimensions of space but also according to dimensions of time: Each époque [epoch] and each group has its own forms of anti-Americanism. In the 20th century, much of this criticism focused on the economic aspect of U.S. cultural exports. In the 21st century, it seems, people around the world worry more about the global political implications of American power.

In the Cold War, French anti-Americanism originated in the rift between communism and socialism. Public debates denounced American expansionism, NATO [the North Atlantic Treaty Organization], and what was seen as the corruptive influence of American art, all of which horrified French elites but not the mass of voters. Instead, the "American Way of Life" fascinated a generation of young French in love with consumerism, better living standards, and economic growth.

The French case is instructive because it points to the most fundamental paradox of cultural anti-Americanism: At any point in time this criticism was and is unthinkable without the flipside, philo-Americanism [love of American culture]. The tension between the two represents the very condition necessary to support the existence of both: High expectations and bitter disillusion are always joined at the hip.

Power Generates Suspicion

Still, most powerful states have experienced the basic historical lesson that power generates suspicion, and the more power a dominant nation exerts the more antagonistic other nations turn. In the interwar period [between the world wars] and even during the early Cold War years, a number of political and cultural observers grasped this point, and they alerted U.S. policymakers to the consequences of this development. As the United States became a world superpower, it was inevitable that people abroad, in the words of American theologian Reinhold Niebuhr, would "hate those who hold power over them"—this is true in both cultural and political terms. When pondering the future of globalization and the role the United States will play in this context, we may wish to remember the words of this wise man.

Periodical Bibliography

The following articles have been selected to supplement the diverse views presented in this chapter.

Martha Bayles	"The Return of Cultural Diplomacy," *Newsweek*, December 31, 2008.
James Vaughn Bowman	"The Mystification of Change," *New Criterion*, January 2009.
Danny Duncan Collum	"'We Are the World': Now Playing Near You: A Global Monoculture," *Sojourners*, May 2007.
Mark Edmundson	"Notes on Mono-Culture," *Massachusetts Review*, Spring–Summer 2009.
Boris Kachka	"What the World Thinks About Us," *Conde Nast Traveler*, November 2008.
Andrew Kohut and Richard Wike	"Positive Aspects of U.S. Image," *Harvard International Review*, Winter 2009.
Ambardar Rekha	"America's Popularity Potion," *World & I*, October 2007.
William Triplett	"U.S. Needs Image Tuck," *Variety*, December 24, 2007.
Mortimer B. Zuckerman	"What Sets Us Apart," *U.S. News & World Report*, July 3, 2006.

For Further Discussion

Chapter 1

1. Blogging is a popular pursuit that appeals to a broad section of the world's population. After examining the evidence given in the viewpoints by Howard Owens and Michael Skube, defend your own view of the role blogging plays in delivering news and opinion to the Internet audience. Specifically address the issue of writing quality displayed on blog sites and whether you think blogging heralds the future of journalism.

2. Reality-based television has dominated the programming of major cable and network channels in recent times. Michael Hirschorn claims that reality TV is popular because it offers an alternative to dramatic and comedic formulas employed in fictional programs. He further believes that it is engaging because it often addresses real social issues that affect viewers. James Wolcott maintains that reality TV caters to viewers' lowest interests, including voyeurism and the desire to feel superior to others. Whose argument do you find more convincing? Use your own experience of reality television to explain your view. For instance, do you prefer certain reality shows over others? Why or why not?

Chapter 2

1. The first three viewpoints in Chapter 2 address the evolution of television as a result of Internet video Web sites. Reread the viewpoints and give your opinion about video streaming sites such as YouTube and Hulu. Are these sites in any way beneficial to society, as argued by Mick O'Leary? Do you believe, as Bob X. Cringely does, that

Internet television will eventually supplant traditional cable television? Why or why not? Are fears that sites like these will assume greater importance and replace television misplaced, as suggested by Patrick West? Use quotes from the viewpoints to support your answers.

2. While often criticized as a site where individuals post utterly mundane information, such as what they are eating for breakfast, instances of Twitter's use in matters of much greater importance, including the revolts following the summer 2009 elections in Iran, have led some champions of the site to tout its cultural and social significance. Reread viewpoints 4 and 5 and construct your own opinion about Twitter. Do you believe it can be used as a catalyst for societal change or is it culturally useless? If you have a Twitter account, does your use of the site coincide with your view? Why or why not?

Chapter 3

1. In the pair of viewpoints on violence in video games, the authors take opposing sides on the debate about whether this fictional violence influences real-world violence. On what evidence does Amanda Schaffer base her argument? On what evidence does Torrey Meeks base his claims? Whose opinion do you find more credible, and which element or elements of the argument did you find most convincing?

2. After reading the viewpoints by Deborah A. Fisher and Jonathan Freedman, describe how you would limit children from accessing too much violence on television. Be sure to examine the methods (for example, restricting viewing to prime time hours, ratings, and the use of a V-chip) that networks have already tried in forming your argument. Also explain what your proposal—which could include some or all of the methods already in use—would accomplish.

Chapter 4

1. The first viewpoint in Chapter 4 discusses international perceptions of the United States as a result of its popular culture exports. Robert Royal has a fairly negative perception of American pop culture's influence on other countries and their view of America as a result. Reread the viewpoint and give your opinion of the author's ideas about American pop culture. Do you agree with the assessment that it distorts the international view of America? Conduct some additional outside research to determine whether the author's claims about negative views of America in light of it's cultural exports are in fact widespread. Finally, consider whether Royal's religious background impacts his views.

2. Viewpoints 3 and 5 in this chapter present the views of an American and a European, respectively, on American pop culture and its effect on the world. Elizabeth Lev, an American living in Rome, discusses the increasing use of American profanity by Europeans as evidence that the negative aspects of American pop culture are distorting foreign perceptions of the United States. Jessica C.E. Gienow-Hecht maintains that popular culture is not as responsible for negative views of America as is America's position as the world's sole superpower. Is it naïve for an American to think that popular culture is of such great importance that it could have such a negative influence on international perceptions of the country? Does this line of thinking reveal a fundamental misunderstanding on the part of the American people regarding how the country is viewed by the global society? Explain.

3. American popular culture is generally believed to have an overarching influence on countries worldwide. In this chapter, the second and fourth viewpoints address American pop culture's current global dominance. Both Tyler Cowen and Richard Pells see its prominence waning. Re-

read these viewpoints in the context of the other viewpoints in this chapter and decide whether you think American popular culture is really less influential now than in past decades. Use quotes from the viewpoints throughout the chapter to support your arguments.

Organizations to Contact

The editors have compiled the following list of organizations concerned with the issues debated in this book. The descriptions are derived from materials provided by the organizations. All have publications or information available for interested readers. The list was compiled on the date of publication of the present volume; the information provided here may change. Be aware that many organizations take several weeks or longer to respond to inquiries, so allow as much time as possible.

Americana: The Institute for the Study of American Popular Culture
7095-1240 Hollywood Blvd., Hollywood, CA 90028-8903
e-mail: editor@americanpopularculture.com
Web site: www.americanpopularculture.com

Americana is a nonprofit institute seeking to empower and uplift humanity through the publication of essays and writings that embody the ideals of American creative writing and scholarship. The organization collects twentieth and twenty-first century American pop culture works and publishes the articles in one of three periodicals *Magazine Americana, Americana: The Journal of American Popular Culture, 1900–Present*, and *Review Americana: A Literary Journal*. The Americana Web site provides many of these articles online, organized by topic, including film, television, music, and sports.

Center for Media Literacy (CML)
23852 Pacific Coast Hwy., #472, Malibu, CA 90265
(310) 456-1225 • fax: (310) 456-0020
e-mail: cml@medialit.org
Web site: www.medialit.org

CML seeks to increase critical analysis of the media through its publication of educational materials and "Medialit Kits." CML was founded on the belief that media literacy is an essential skill in the twenty-first century as varying media forms become increasingly omnipresent in everyday life, and on the belief that individuals should be empowered from a young age to make informed choices about the media they consume. *Connections* is the official newsletter of the organization, with archival issues available online. Additional informative materials can be browsed by topic on the CML Web site.

Center for Screen-Time Awareness (CSTA)

1200 Twenty-ninth St. NW, Lower Level #1
Washington, DC   20007
(202) 333-9220 • fax: (202) 333-9221
e-mail: cfstaemail@screentime.org
Web site: www.screentime.org

Throughout its history CSTA has undergone numerous name changes but has remained focused on encouraging families and communities to remain connected by limiting their exposure to and dependence on modern electronic media. The organization sponsors Turnoff Week, in which families are asked to turn off their televisions, computers, and other media (such as iPods and cell phones), with the goal of encouraging the participation in more-engaging family activities. Additional information about current campaigns as well as fact sheets about current use of electronic media can be found on the CSTA Web site.

Entertainment Software Ratings Board (ESRB)

317 Madison Ave., 22nd Fl., New York, NY   10017
Web site: www.esrb.org

ESRB was founded in 1994 to be the self-regulating body for the video game industry. The board has been charged with multiple duties, including determining content-based ratings for computer and video games, enforcing advertising guidelines set by the industry, and ensuring online privacy practices for Internet gaming. The ESRB was created to aid all consumers, especially families, in making appropriate decisions about

Organizations to Contact

which games to purchase. Additional information about the ratings system and current projects by the ESRB can be found on the organization's Web site.

Federal Communications Commission (FCC)
445 Twelfth St. SW, Washington, DC   20554
(888) 225-5322 • fax: (888) 418-0232
e-mail: fccinfo@fcc.gov
Web site: www.fcc.gov

Established as part of the Communications Act of 1934, the FCC is an independent agency within the U.S. government in charge of overseeing national and international radio, television, wire, satellite, and cable communications. Headed by five commissioners appointed by the president, the commission publishes annual reports, updates, and reviews about the state of communications and regulations in the country. Overviews summarizing current legislation governing the communications industry are provided on the agency's Web site.

Focus on the Family
8605 Explorer Dr., Colorado Springs, CO   80920
(800) 232-6459
Web site: www.focusonthefamily.com

Focus on the Family is a Christian organization dedicated to the promotion of traditional family values both nationally and internationally. Through a combination of radio and Internet broadcasts, diverse publications, and conferences, Focus on the Family works to inspire married couples worldwide to maintain their family and raise their children according to Christian beliefs. Often critical of popular culture, this organization offers writings elucidating its concerns about the value of contemporary pop culture. Publications include "The Influence of MTV," "The Lost Ethics of Pop Culture," and "Innocence Lost."

Free Expression Policy Project (FEPP)

170 W. Seventy-sixth St., #301, New York, NY   10023
Web site: www.fepproject.org

With its founding in 2000, FEPP began work to advocate for free speech, copyright regulation, and democracy in the media. The organization's work focuses on restrictions on publically funded projects, Internet filters and ratings systems, copyright laws, corporate media consolidation, and censorship. Unwilling to take an absolutist stance on any of these issues, FEPP examines issues relating to the media and popular culture as they are raised and seeks to provide a balanced assessment of each of these topics of inquiry. The FEPP Web site offers reports and commentary covering issues such as the Internet, media policy, and violence in the media.

Media Coalition

275 Seventh Ave., Suite 1504, New York, NY   10001
(212) 587-4025 • fax: (212) 587-2436
Web site: www.mediacoalition.org

The Media Coalition represents a wide range of media publishers in the United States, including the Association of American Publishers, the Motion Picture Association of America, and the Recording Industry Association of America, among others. The organization's stated goal is two-pronged: to defend the First Amendment right to publish and sell all forms of media, and to defend the American public's right to consume that media. The coalition opposes restrictive legislation placed on media publishers by the government, and participates in litigation efforts to suppress the passage of such laws. Reports on the Media Coalition's current efforts can be read online.

National Cable & Telecommunications Association (NCTA)

25 Massachusetts Ave. NW, Ste. 100, Washington, DC   20001
(202) 222-2300
Web site: www.ncta.com

As the trade association of the cable industry, the NCTA provides the national, unified voice on all issues affecting companies in the cable and telecommunications fields. With its reports and lobbying programs, the association seeks to influence policy governing the cable industry. Issues addressed by the organization include Internet access, parental controls, and video competition, with reports on these topics and others available on the NCTA Web site.

Parents Television Council (PTC)

707 Wilshire Blvd., #2075, Los Angeles, CA   90017
(213) 403-1300
e-mail: editor@parentstv.org
Web site: www.parentstv.org

The PTC was founded with the goal of limiting children's exposure to violence, sex, and profanity in television programming and other media. The council works closely with federal legislators to create and enforce legislation to ensure that children are not bombarded with harmful messages when watching television. In addition to its annual *Family Guide to Prime Time Television*, the PTC Web site offers reviews of individual television shows and movies. Additional publications about the state of media in the United States as well as proposed legislation can be accessed online as well.

Popular Culture: Resources for Critical Analysis

American Studies, PO Box 644013
Washington State University, Pullman, WA   99164
(509) 335-1560
e-mail: reedtv@wsu.edu
Web site: www.wsu.edu/~amerstu/pop/tvguide.html

Popular Culture: Resources for Critical Analysis is a Web site created by Washington State University history professor T.V. Reed in conjunction with his American Popular Culture course. The site provides many articles and links to aid in the critical analysis of popular culture, focusing not only on its national impact, but on the international ramifications as well. Issues highlighted on the site include race, ethnicity, class, and censorship among others.

Popular Culture Association/American Culture Association (PCA/ACA)

267 Bessey Hall, East Lansing, MI   48824
(517) 355-6660 • fax: (517) 355-5250
Web site: www.pcaaca.org

PCA/ACA is a consortium of American popular culture scholars and enthusiasts who work together to define and analyze popular culture in the United States today. The organization publishes two journals, *Journal of Popular Culture* and the *Journal of American Culture*. Each publication offers a more in-depth understanding of American life and culture by combining traditional history studies with scholastically ignored aspects of American life, such as pop culture. The PCA/ACA Web site provides additional information about popular culture and its impact on American life.

Bibliography of Books

John Alberti   *Text Messaging: Reading and Writing
                      About Popular Culture*. Florence, KY:
                      Wadsworth, 2008.

LeRoy Ashby   *With Amusement for All: A History of
                      American Popular Culture Since 1830*.
                      Lexington: University Press of
                      Kentucky, 2006.

Ben H. Bagdikian   *The New Media Monopoly*. Boston:
                      Beacon, 2004.

Ray B. Browne   *Profiles of Popular Culture: A Reader*.
                      Madison, WI: Popular, 2005.

Jean Burgess and   *YouTube: Online Video and
Joshua Green   Participatory Culture*. Cambridge:
                      Polity, 2009.

Lane Crothers   *Globalization and American Popular
                      Culture*. 2nd ed. Lanham, MD:
                      Rowman & Littlefield, 2009.

Shirley Fedorak   *Pop Culture: The Culture of Everyday
                      Life*. Toronto: UTP Higher Education,
                      2009.

Nathan W. Fisk   *Understanding Online Piracy: The
                      Truth About Illegal File Sharing*. Santa
                      Barbara, CA: ABC-CLIO, 2009.

Jib Fowles   *The Case for Television Violence*.
                      Newbury Park, CA: Sage, 1999.

Matthew Fraser   *Weapons of Mass Distraction: Soft
                      Power and American Empire*. New
                      York: Thomas Dunne, 2005.

Joshua Gamson   *Claims to Fame: Celebrity in Contemporary America.* Berkeley and Los Angeles: University of California Press, 1994.

James Paul Gee   *What Video Games Have to Teach Us About Learning and Literacy.* 2nd ed. New York: Palgrave Macmillan, 2007.

Dave Grossman and Gloria Degaetano   *Stop Teaching Our Kids to Kill: A Call to Action Against TV, Movie and Video Game Violence.* New York: Crown, 1999.

Keith Gumery   *International Views: America and the Rest of the World.* New York: Longman, 2006.

James T. Hamilton   *Channeling Violence.* Princeton, NJ: Princeton University Press, 2000.

Andrew Hammond   *Popular Culture in the Arab World.* Cairo, Egypt: American University in Cairo Press, 2007.

Su Holmes and Deborah Jermyn, eds.   *Understanding Reality Television.* New York: Routledge, 2004.

Peter Howe   *Paparazzi: And Our Obsession with Celebrity.* New York: Artisan, 2005.

Mizuko Ito et al.   *Hanging Out, Messing Around, and Geeking Out: Kids Living and Learning with New Media.* Cambridge, MA: MIT Press, 2009.

Henry Jenkins — *Fans, Bloggers, and Gamers: Media Consumers in a Digital Age.* New York: New York University Press, 2006.

Roland Kelts — *Japanamerica: How Japanese Pop Culture Has Invaded the U.S.* New York: Palgrave Macmillan, 2007.

Lawrence Kutner — *Grand Theft Childhood: The Surprising Truth About Violent Video Games and What Parents Can Do.* New York: Simon & Schuster, 2008.

Cooper Lawrence — *The Cult of Celebrity: What Our Fascination with the Stars Reveals About Us.* Guilford, CT: Skirt!, 2009.

Antony Loewenstein — *The Blogging Revolution.* Carlton, Australia: Melbourne University Publishing, 2008.

Amanda Lotz — *The Television Will Be Revolutionized.* New York: New York University Press, 2007.

Laurie Ouellette and Susan Murray — *Reality TV: Remaking Television Culture.* 2nd ed. New York: New York University Press, 2008.

Neil Postman — *Amusing Ourselves to Death: Public Discourse in the Age of Show Business.* 20th anniversary ed. New York: Penguin, 2005.

Marc Prensky — *Don't Bother Me, Mom—I'm Learning!* St. Paul, MN: Paragon House, 2006.

Scott Rosenberg — *Say Everything: How Blogging Began, What It's Becoming, and Why It Matters*. New York: Crown, 2009.

Jonathan Silverman and Dean Rader — *The World Is a Text: Writing, Reading and Thinking About Visual and Popular Culture*. 3rd ed. Upper Saddle River, NJ: Prentice-Hall, 2008.

C. John Sommerville — *How the News Makes Us Dumb: The Death of Wisdom in an Information Society*. Downers Grove, IL: InterVarsity Press, 1999.

Karen Sternheimer — *It's Not the Media: The Truth About Pop Culture's Influence on Children*. New York: Basic Books, 2003.

John Storey — *Cultural Theory and Popular Culture: An Introduction*. 4th ed. Athens: University of Georgia Press, 2006.

Wallace Wang — *Steal This File Sharing Book*. San Francisco: No Starch Press, 2004.

Index